Why Europe Fears Its Neighbors

Why Europe Fears Its Neighbors

Fabrizio Tassinari

PRAEGER SECURITY INTERNATIONAL
An Imprint of ABC-CLIO, LLC

A B C 🔅 C L I O

Santa Barbara, California • Denver, Colorado • Oxford, England

Library of Congress Cataloging-in-Publication Data

Tassinari, Fabrizio.
  Why Europe fears its neighbors / Fabrizio Tassinari.
    p. cm.
  Includes bibliographical references and index.
  ISBN 978-0-313-35772-5 (hard copy : alk. paper) —
ISBN 978-0-313-35773-2 (ebook) 1. European Union countries—
Foreign relations. I. Title.
  JZ1570.T37 2009
  327.4—dc22   2009021939

13 12 11 10 9 1 2 3 4 5

This book is also available on the World Wide Web as an eBook.
Visit www.abc-clio.com for details.

ABC-CLIO, LLC
130 Cremona Drive, P.O. Box 1911
Santa Barbara, California 93116-1911

This book is printed on acid-free paper ∞

Manufactured in the United States of America

For William, at last

How many times, within thy memory,
Customs, and laws, and coins, and offices
Have been by thee renew'd, and people changed.
If thou remember'st well and canst see clear,
Thou wilt perceive thyself like a sick wretch,
Who finds no rest upon her down, but oft
Shifting her side, short respite seeks from pain.

    Dante Alighieri, *The Divine Comedy*, Purgatory, Canto VI

Contents

Introduction: Thy Neighbor, Thyself   1

1   Where Europe Is Not   9

2   The Path to Normalcy   27

3   Turkish Ironies   41

4   The Remains of the Wall   53

5   Russia's Roller Coaster   67

6   A Sea of Troubles   79

7   The Wide West   91

Conclusion: A Sensible Europe   103

Acknowledgments   117

Notes   121

Index   137

Introduction

Thy Neighbor, Thyself

On the face of it, this is not a book about Europe. It is about countries and regions neighboring the European Union (EU): the Balkans, Turkey, the westernmost former Soviet republics, Russia, and the Mediterranean area. It is about extreme poverty, nationalism, open war—the sort of issues that Europeans have long considered buried in their dustbin of history. On the face of it, this is a book about places and problems that are extraneous to the path of peace and prosperity that Europe has followed over the past six decades.

All the same, the European backyard is as good a place as any to observe Europe. These countries and regions may not always be or feel unequivocally "European," but in most cases they aspire to come closer to—or even be part of—modern Europe. Their relationship with the EU will define the ultimate shape and boundaries of the political constellation of Europe. From immigration to energy dependence, Europe's neighbors are host to challenges that many Europeans would rather want to avert; and yet, those very challenges are shaping 21st-century Europe. This book concerns what Europe is no longer, but it is really about what Europe wants to become.

Consider, indeed, immigration and energy. The total immigrant community in Europe has reached some 44 million, 30 percent of which are estimated to come from neighboring countries. The largest communities of immigrants living in Europe hail from Turkey, Morocco, Albania, and Algeria—all European neighbors. Many of the others come from or through Eastern Europe, North Africa, and the Balkans, at a rate of some 2 million new entries each year.[1] One way of weighing these figures would be to measure them against the aging European population or its anemic labor markets. However, in the increasingly heated political discourse pervading Western Europe, immigration is more commonly tied to the religious orientation of migrants, to the crime rates or levels of education in Europe's degraded suburbia.

Europe imports approximately 50 percent of the hydrocarbons that it consumes—a figure that the EU[*] foresees increasing to 70 percent by 2030. Most of the arteries feeding the European oil and gas dependency originate in Algeria, Libya, the Gulf monarchies, Azerbaijan, and Russia. Countries such as Ukraine, Turkey, Belarus, and Georgia are crucial for transit. European countries may be trying to kick their gasoline habit through wide-ranging environmental measures. But they have surely not yet been able to overcome their addiction to lucrative energy deals with their autocratic neighbors.

Immigration and energy may be emblematic, but they are the tip of the iceberg. Speaking of autocracies, the majority of Europe's neighbors are not governed by stable and functioning liberal democracies. The Bertelsmann Transformation Index, which measures the state of market-based democracy worldwide, cites "deficiencies," "unfavourable preconditions," and "serious obstacles" throughout Europe's backyard. In the survey on political rights and civil liberties published by the organization Freedom House, none of the countries in North Africa and the former Soviet Union—with the debatable exception of Ukraine—are categorized as "fully free."

The European neighborhood is also one large powder keg of dormant or open conflicts. From the Caucasus to Cyprus, some of these are decades-old confrontations exacerbated by religion or ethnicity; others are splinters of the post-1989 geopolitical disorder. In all cases, the result has been endemic instability and a mosaic of self-proclaimed statelets and isolated enclaves. These conflicts have generated millions of internally displaced persons and refugees[2] and proven a fertile ground for a range of illegal activities that already flourish across the periphery of Europe.

To the extent that a single European psyche actually exists, it is not difficult to fathom the images conjured up by this state of affairs. Spaniards and Italians cannot turn their backs on the relentless broadcasting of boatloads of Africans landing on their southern shores. Some Lithuanians and Czechs must have had unpleasant flashbacks when hearing the stiff Russian official informing them about the closure of their oil tap.

To the extent that these images can be quantified, the overall impression is that Europeans are alarmed by their neighbors. Recent polls suggest that two out of three Europeans are concerned about Russia as an energy provider and about Moscow's behavior

---

[*]All too often, especially within Europe, the EU has come to "copyright" the meaning of Europe and the terms are used interchangeably. Although inevitable to some extent, common EU institutions do not always embody or speak for "Europe," and there is much more to Europe than just the EU. Whenever the choice is plainly discernible, in this book I will refer to the EU when dealing more generally and collectively with European countries and peoples that are also part of the EU or when referring to the historical and philosophical nation of Europe.

towards its neighbors. About 70 percent in Germany and France believe that Turkey has such different values that it cannot be considered a Western country. Two-thirds of the population in Italy, the Netherlands, and Spain think that greater interaction between the Muslim and Western worlds constitutes a threat.[3] Name one of the countries neighboring Europe, and it is quite likely that the average European citizen will at best associate it with gaping cultural or economic differences and at worst with the barbarians at the gate.

Nonetheless, there is something that surveys cannot grasp, figures cannot capture, and that the European psyche can all too easily overlook: Europe has always had these neighbors. Europeans have met, clashed, joined forces in battle, and crushed their neighbors for centuries. All the while that Russia was fighting Napoleon, its political and cultural establishment was primarily French-speaking. The constant menace posed by the Ottomans fortified the Christian identity of Europe. During the Middle Ages, it was Islam that preserved many works from classical antiquity, and yet it was also during the Middle Ages that the Crusades took place.

The interface between Europe and its neighbors has been shaped in space and time, by territorial contiguity, and centuries of interdependence. Whether that interface is cooperative or conflictual is as much up to Europe as it is to its neighbors. The political, societal, and economic predicament in the European backyard is serious. But the magnitude of the test only becomes fully comprehensible when considering also Europe itself.

THE NEXUS THAT COULD

As is often the case, *The Economist* said it best. In October 2004, the British magazine ran an editorial titled, "How terrorism trumped federalism."[4] The article dealt primarily with the debate on Turkish accession to the EU, but the title of the piece says much more. It crystallizes the extent to which Europe's paramount quest for security (of which the fight against terrorism is but one facet) thwarts its equally vital process of integration (as incarnated to the utmost degree by the notion of federalism).

Security and integration, or to be precise, the correlation between security and integration, has been at the heart of the post-World War II European project. That greatest of feats, rendering war between European countries impossible, has been attained through the relentless quest for integration pursued by everyone, from the architects of the Marshall Plan to the creators of the Euro, Europe's single currency. The balance of power that dominated European geopolitics for centuries never succeeded in bringing lasting peace to Europe; that has been accomplished by gradual integration, the pooling of resources, and the voluntary sharing of sovereignty.

The rationale of this mechanism is distinctive for its disarming simplicity. The more countries share in common, the less likely it becomes that they will attack one another. The result has been so path-breaking as to appear almost counterintuitive: Instead of defending themselves by closing their borders and erecting barriers, European nations have sought stability by opening up to one another.

Integration has been the European response to every major shift in the geopolitical constellation of Europe. The end of dictatorships in Greece, Spain, and Portugal as well as the collapse of the Soviet Union each led to a "widening," as it is called, of the European integration process, in the form of enlargements of the EU to include the countries of Southern and Central Europe. Each widening has corresponded with a "deepening" in the form of a series of treaties aimed at creating a more integrated Europe. In Europe, integration *is* security, and this nexus has been constitutive of what Europe is today.

The correlation of security and integration in Europe has defined a peculiar system of international governance based upon shared rules and sophisticated institutions. It has led to a common European narrative that has emerged alongside the national identities of the participating countries and peoples. It has broadened the meaning of what is domestic and what is foreign. The free zone passport and the Euro are domestic issues, while the EU has acquired a growing presence in foreign policy alongside that of its member states.

Europe's neighbors present a challenge to all this. Different peoples, cultures, and traditions can elicit anything from curiosity to skepticism to defensiveness. One of the principle tasks facing the EU has been that of repeatedly demonstrating its ability to embrace different nations in a broader political framework. One of its most outstanding accomplishments has been the reproduction of its foundational nexus of security and integration in new regions and countries of Europe. As top European diplomat Robert Cooper has argued, the EU has proven able and willing to "enlarge the context."[5]

In today's neighborhood, however, Europe appears to have stretched this context to the point of breaking it altogether. Instead of nurturing its original correlation, the European approach towards its current neighbors actually separates security from integration.

Peace and stability are not pursued through the gradual inclusion of the periphery. Integration is no longer about whether and how to bring neighboring countries close to the EU, but mostly about how to rescue cooperation within an already heterogeneous Union. Europe is decoupling its quest for security and that for wider integration, and by doing so, fails to attain either of them.

IMAGE AND REALITY

To an outsider, European countries frequently appear divided on major strategic issues. The foreign policy of the EU seems ineffectual and ambivalent. The overall European posture often comes out as irritating—when not outright hypocritical. Nowhere is this more evident than in the European neighborhood. The EU enlargement process has turned out to be hugely successful. Especially in the case of the former communist countries that entered the EU in 2004, the lure of membership represented the best incentive to accompany the political and economic transition of these countries. Their domestic transformation provided the means for the EU to stabilize the region. And the overall European political and diplomatic profile emerged enormously strengthened.

The inclusion of more impoverished countries was always bound to raise concerns in Western European quarters. European citizens soon began voicing these concerns, ranging from the outsourcing of European companies and jobs to a feared invasion of Slavic immigrants. The first casualties of this inward-looking mood are inevitably the countries now queuing up for EU membership: the seven Balkan states and Turkey. For all of them, the prospects of entering Europe are still alive. Some of them, like Croatia, may manage to make the cut and join the EU quite soon. Even so, not one week goes by without some European government warning that the EU is not ready for further enlargements, or that some of the candidate countries are too volatile, too poor, or—not infrequently—too Muslim to enter the EU.

Those neighbors in the former Soviet Union and the Mediterranean region, for which the EU does not hold out prospects of entry, have not been spared by this widespread introspection. For them, the EU has devised an impressive range of policy instruments and poured out substantial sums in financial assistance. If possible, however, the paradox here is even more puzzling. The EU claims to attract these neighbors, while it is careful to keep them at arm's length from Europe. It seeks to draw them closer, but it refrains from offering them the most attractive incentives. Europe's neighborhood strategy is fraught with ambiguity.

The security–integration nexus provides a privileged, albeit not at all reassuring, perspective from which to consider this quandary. The expansion of the EU has been groundbreaking because the EU has given its new members a stake in the future of European peace. Enlargement is about the security consumer that becomes a security provider, the insured becoming the insurer; it is ultimately about the celebration of a different political and social entity born out of this transformation.

The trouble with this strategy is that enlargement will exhaust itself at some point. The EU cannot continue to expand indefinitely and must end somewhere. Europe cannot escape its quest for security, yet security cannot be attained through an ever-wider expansion of the EU. The most immediate remedy against looming instability is, then, to keep threats away and countries outside. The only apparent way out is to be locked in a "Fortress Europe." Europe's instinctive reaction to the enlargement neuralgia has been to withdraw into itself.

On the surface, it is easy to mistake this for one of Europe's recurrent crises of confidence. All too often, it seems as though the European response to major strategic questions consists of evading answers until solutions somehow sort themselves out. By shutting its neighbors out, however, the EU is backtracking on the very foundations of modern Europe. The message that the EU is sending to the world and to its own citizens is that the process of continental integration is no longer Europe's revolutionary recipe for peace. For lack of plausible alternatives to expansion, Europe reverts to pursuing stability by means of exclusion. What on the surface appears to be another instance of ambiguity is in reality the most palpable sign of deep angst about the future of Europe. By shutting its neighbors out, the EU is undermining the very pillars upon which it was established.

THE CLOSING RING

The 2003 European Security Strategy—the nearest the European countries have come to a collective security doctrine—proclaims that the EU seeks to "promote a ring of well-governed countries to the East of the European Union and on the borders of the Mediterranean with whom we can enjoy close and cooperative relations."[6] If reality has yet to reflect these noble aspirations, it is because

Europe's neighbors are proving to be the most decisive test for Europe as a polity, institution, and power constellation.

This is not to say that Europe is a delusional conclave of countries locked in its own ''post-historical'' oasis of peace. Nor is it to imply that getting the neighborhood right is part of a march to ''Europeanize'' the world.[7] Europe is neither inexorably doomed to decline nor is it likely to ''master'' global developments, as some Europeans like to put it. Europe is one of the world regions that feels most pressured by globalization, whether because of its stagnant demography or its unease with multiculturalism. However, it is also the region that, by creating the most cohesive model of regional integration, has in many ways anticipated globalization.

The neighbors are Europe's miniature globalization. Like globalization, the European periphery is ultimately about a relentless flow of information and ideas, people and cultures, in and out of Europe. And that flow can quickly turn into instability, violence, and chaos. Just like globalization, the European neighborhood presents the EU with huge economic opportunities and vulnerabilities. European countries are by far the top trade partners throughout this region. And yet, one of the many lessons painfully taught by the financial and economic maelstrom that started in 2008 is how quickly and profoundly instability can engulf a whole region, as has been the case in Eastern Europe. For better or worse, American scholars Daniel Hamilton and Joseph Quinlan have a point in arguing that ''Europe's got its China next door.''[8]

Europe's neighbors—and the challenges emanating from them—are so diverse that the very reference to a ''European neighborhood'' may seem excessively Euro-centric. The phrase, however, is not justified by Europe supposedly acting as an irresistible magnet for these countries. It is motivated by the fact that these neighbors are all in different ways shaping the contours of tomorrow's Europe.

From the Balkans and Eastern Europe, to North Africa and the Middle East, this book will explain how security concerns define Europe's posture, its policies, and its very identity. It will examine the role that Turkey and Russia claim in the European power architecture and the impact that these countries have on Europe's self-perception. It will look at the United States, in its own way Europe's paramount neighbor, but more importantly, the one country that can still single-handedly alter the power constellation in the wider European continent.

Many an observer has complained that Europe is not where it is supposed to be.[9] The EU has grown in size, its ambition has swelled, and its political project has evolved beyond recognition. Yet, Europe has plunged into an identity crisis that is coming at the cost of its hard-won legitimacy and of its most basic attainments of peace, democracy, and prosperity.

Exploring Europe's relations with its neighbors is not merely about reclaiming that legitimacy and again pursuing those attainments. It is about nothing less than looking for Europe where it is not expected to be.

1

Where Europe Is Not

Mani was born and died in Mesopotamia. While that ought to make perfect sense, in hindsight it would sooner appear to be one of history's bitter coincidences. It ought to make sense, because some 1,800 years ago Mesopotamia was a land of contrasts. It was where the Roman Empire faded into the Persian one; where religions came together, cultures overlapped, and languages mixed. Mani wandered across this scattered land and beyond, preaching his views about the world, the human condition, and the afterlife. He saw the universe as a struggle between light and darkness; God and Matter; body and soul. He claimed that these opposites are eternally conflicting while being inextricably connected.

Hardly anything that Mani actually said has reached us, and his life and work are the stuff for historians of religion.[1] Nevertheless, he is survived by an adjective that we have adopted and continue to use to this day. "Manichaean," says the *Oxford English Dictionary*, is something or someone "characterized by dualistic contrast or conflict between opposites." That can be regarded as a virtue if you prize strong principles, resolve, and tenacity. In most cases, however, it borders on the insulting, implying a stubborn aversion to compromises, together with an inability to see shades of gray.

Today's Europe is characterized by something akin to this usage of the term—and it is neither a blessing nor a curse. What Europe is and what it does originate from a sort of inherent, although often unconscious, dualism. The continent's post-war integration project has been the most extraordinary outcome of an existential contrast about the very meaning of Europe and of a relentless quest to rise above it. For all its achievements, one serious misunderstanding about Europe has been that of deeming the continent's dialectic nature redundant.

All this is at the core of the gargantuan challenge and opportunity presented by the countries and regions neighboring Europe, and this is also where the Mesopotamian connection returns—as history's bitter coincidence.

IN FEAR WE TRUST

In May 2003, Jürgen Habermas and Jacques Derrida, two of Europe's most illustrious thinkers, penned a provocative newspaper article.[2] They chose to examine Europe through the Manichaean struggle of our time: the "war on terror" and, more specifically, the U.S.-led war in Iraq. This was the war of the "with us or with the terrorists"; the war pitted "New" Europe against the "Old" one, as then U.S. Defense Secretary Donald Rumsfeld put it. It inflamed the Muslim world with hatred against the West, tarnished the global image of the United States, and estranged Europe from its long-time U.S. ally.

Habermas and Derrida, however, did not view the war in Iraq solely as a destructive event. On the contrary, they saw it as a defining formative moment for Europe; to be precise, the birth of a new European subject that is ready, willing, and equipped to lead the world in a more just and tolerant direction. To make their case, they produced convincing evidence: the multitude of Europeans who took to the streets of their respective capital cities on February 15th of that year in order to express their opposition to the war and voice their desire for peace.

Not even in the darkest days of the occupation of Iraq was everyone in Europe with the two great intellectuals on this one. Anti-Americanism is hardly new in some Western European circles, and the argument forwarded by Habermas and Derrida struck as merely a sophisticated version of this sentiment. Beneath the surface, however, their "plea" had little to do with the United States and represented the latest edition of a *leitmotiv* that has accompanied Europe for ages.

To define themselves and the challenges ahead of them, Europeans have always sought an opposite. This opposite—the "other," to use a term that was formerly confined to identity studies[3]—needs not necessarily be an adversary, but for Europe the extraordinary fact is that it has been a constructive force. It has held up a mirror that has presented Europe with its aspirations and achievements, as much as it has confronted it with its flaws and failures. This opposite has shown Europe what have become its most entrenched values.

The deepest "other" of contemporary Europe is as dreadful as it is ordinary: its own past.[4] Today, Europeans watch their respective national teams facing one another in a continent-wide soccer tournament. They hear coaches and players speak of battles, survival, and honor when explaining their jobs. They see hordes of idolizing fans chanting marches; the French citizens call to arms while the Italians vow to fight till death. Until little over half a century ago, Europeans actually meant that. They heard their political leaders declaring war, armies fought one another, and Europeans killed each other by the millions. They certainly did not need a soccer field to vent their nationalist instincts.

After 1945, Europe's per capita income was about 40 percent of the U.S. average. From 1950 to the first oil shock in 1973, average gross domestic product (GDP) growth in Western Europe approached rates of 5 percent a year, with China-style peaks in West Germany in the early post-war years of 8–10 percent.[5] By the 1980s, Europeans had to cope with their infamous "butter mountains" and "wine lakes" resulting from production in excess of the agreed-upon quotas. As we will see, poverty has not been eradicated from the European continent and the prospects of the European economy are not particularly rosy. Yet, this unrelenting rejection of the past has provided a rationale for the unprecedented—and in many ways unrepeatable—recovery that Western European economies underwent during the first post-war decades.

The then-and-now exercise is probably most revealing when considering the political transformation of Europe. Today, we are told, Belarus is the last dictatorship in Europe. When EU members or candidate countries provide the tiniest indication of making a shift away from democracy, like Austria or Slovakia did in the late-1990s, European countries and institutions are quick to ostracize them. Nevertheless, as historian Timothy Garton Ash has recalled, in 1942 "there were only four perilously free countries in Europe: Britain, Switzerland, Sweden and Ireland."[6] The rest of the Continent was arguably not much freer than today's Belarus.

Peace, prosperity, and democracy may be taken for granted today, but they have only been possible thanks to Europe's escape from its own past. Incidentally, the United States not only made available much of the material resources that enabled Europe to attain these feats. It also provided a number of crucial insights as to how to attain them.

Thanks to U.S. military protection and to the creation of the North Atlantic Treaty Organization (NATO), the countries of Europe could enjoy what is often referred to as a "free ride" for their defense. The Marshall Plan fed the European economic recovery. And it was certainly thanks to the Plan—worth some $200 billion in current figures—that Europeans could kick-start their integration project. The United States insisted on Europeans co-owning the plan's policy-making, scrapping tariff trade barriers, and complying with the system of incentives and conditions that the EU so cherishes today. Washington kept Western Europe at a safe distance from communism and guided it in a direction that Europe had never taken before. The United States, then-Presidential candidate Barack Obama has said, "championed a bold new architecture [that] helped secure the peace."[7]

By the time the Marshall Plan was in full swing, French statesmen Jean Monnet and Robert Schuman were putting the final touches on the 1951 European Coal and Steel Community. Their hunch of linking the French and German economies through these two key materials used in wartime was practical, visionary, and evocative all at the same time. The basic rationale, however, was still that of a "bold new architecture" aimed at securing the peace. The idea was to pool the resources of European nations to such an extent that it becomes inconceivable for them to wage war against one another. It was about capping the upper limits of state sovereignty in order to tame Europe's most destructive impulses. Europeans did something diametrically opposed to what they had ever done before: making interstate integration the foundation of European security.

COMING OF AGE

Since those early exploits, the European project has advanced primarily in response to crises. After the European Defense Community ruinously failed in 1954, faith in the European project was restored through the European Economic Community of 1957. France's "empty chair" tactics and the "Euro-sclerosis" of the 1970s eventually led to the creation of the Single Market in 1987 and to what we now know as the European Union. Any such ride across decades can fall prey to oversimplification. National preferences and bargaining among states and the activism of international actors, including business groups, are all key factors in explaining how the European project has evolved.[8]

Nevertheless, this sort of long-term crisis response is the clearest illustration that—especially in its early years—Europe morphed into an ever-closer union thanks to the attachment and visceral opposition to its own past. Whenever the reluctance or failure to move ahead could take the continent backward, whenever the most likely alternative to more integration was a possible relapse into instability and fragmentation, Europe chose the former.

Also in this respect, 1989 was a watershed year. The fall of the Berlin Wall and the end of the bipolar Cold War–order did provoke a systemic crisis. The year 1989, argued one prominent observer at the time, could have resulted in the "universalization of Western liberal democracy." For others, it could have meant a Europe "more prone to violence" than in the preceding 45 years.[9]

In Western Europe, both options were plausible. In addition to these alternatives, however—and perhaps as a response to them—1989 also meant that Europe was at last free of the straitjacket imposed by the superpowers and able to pursue a purpose of its own. Europe's obsession gradually became less about escaping its past and more about how to turn its break with history into something unique and distinctive. There was at last something "European" that Europe could offer to the world, and 1989 was the crisis that did it.

Any distillation of this supposed European uniqueness is bound to be contentious. Nonetheless, cross-checking some of the eloquent writings on this matter,[10] a few unmistakably European values do surface rather consistently. One feature considered characteristically European is what the Germans call the "social market economy." With some EU states among the most competitive countries worldwide and all of them taken together being the world's largest recipient of foreign direct investment, a social market economy is not to be equated with a rejection of the free market. Yet, Europeans do believe that public institutions exist in order to regulate the market and to provide a number of vital services to its citizens: from free health care and education to comprehensive "cradle-to-grave" welfare systems. In Europe, the state has got to have a "visible hand."

When thinking of the opposite of Europe's social model, it is difficult to deny that the European mind instinctively goes to the United States. Some Europeans despise the U.S. economic and social minimalism as a survival-of-the-fittest type model.[11] Deep down, however, Europe's social market economy again mirrors itself in the continent's own turbulent past. The emergence of the welfare state was tied to World War II because European governments needed to do something to defuse class struggles, social strains, and the rise of nationalism. Historian Tony Judt has explained that during the war "mobilizing men and women for total war meant ... doing whatever was necessary to keep them productive." After it, "some workable balance between political freedom and the rational, equitable distributive function of the administrative state seemed the only sensible route out of the abyss."[12]

The past has also inculcated a firm belief in the rule of law. Roman jurisprudence is part of Europe's genetic code as much as unchecked power—and the abuses of it: from the absolutist monarchies and "l'Etat c'est moi," to the totalitarian dictatorships that pushed Europe into total war. Today, the law is the foundation of the EU governance model, in which sovereignty is limited because member states hold a right of mutual interference based on the same rules of the game. In the same vein, Europeans claim to react to anyone or anything that wants to be more equal than others: whether the prison guard torturing an uncooperative detainee or a government secretly building up its nuclear weapons capacity. That is the rationale of the intricate web of agreements, associations, and partnerships linking the EU with the rest of the world and which Europeans refer to as "effective multilateralism." The rule of law has turned from a strategy for peace in Europe into Europe's strategy for world peace.

A third peculiar European perspective is that, as Habermas and Derrida argue in their resounding appeal: "A president who opens his daily business with public prayer, and associates his significant political decisions with a divine mission, is hard to imagine."[13] This line of argument does not object to the centrality of Judeo-Christianity on Europe, its political thought and moral values. Nor does it contend that the separation of religion and politics is itself uniquely European.

It does, however, capture quite neatly the chief result of one of the most travailed aspects in the emergence of modern Europe. This "privatization of faith" emerged as a consequence of the endless fratricidal conflicts that ravaged the Continent and tore it apart in the Early Modern times, and of the 1,000-year strife between church and state. What is peculiar about the European secular state is that it did not only emerge to shield religion from politics. It emerged to shield politics from religion.

Social market, the rule of law, and the secular state may be all European qualities, but they are also extremely debatable. As the traditional welfare state struggles in Western Europe, new EU members adopt more "minimalist" models. Is there really a "European" social market economy? The countries of Europe, after all, were painfully divided regarding the war in Iraq, so how determined is Europe about international law? And when it comes to the

separation of state and church, what about the differences between
the liberal Anglo-Saxon version emphasizing freedom for all religions and the stricter French *laïcité*, which excludes religion from the
public sphere?

These distinctive features are all the product of Europe's violent
history. But they are not homogeneous, let alone consistently interpreted throughout the continent. It is difficult to see how these
qualities have strengthened the post-Cold War ambition of a more
cohesive and determined Europe. It is hard to detect in them
Europe's original correlation of security and integration. As war-
ranted as they may all be, these objections point straight toward
what has arguably become the most characteristic European
quality.

THE IMPORTANCE OF BEING DIFFERENT

Supporters speak of it as a "powerful weakness." Europe may not
have an army but it has demonstrated its ability to attract and persuade.[14] Detractors may well decry its impotent power. Europe is
rich and developed but destined to irrelevance before other established or rising world powers. Even those who have no strong opinion about Europe cannot overlook that the EU's official motto,
"United in Diversity," looks like an oxymoron.

These expressions may seem elusive, but it is this very vagueness
that is meant to capture the core of contemporary Europe. Europe
has radically overcome its past of divisions and oppositions only by
painstakingly avoiding a situation in which any position would prevail. Europe is not about melting traditions, cultures, and languages
in one large continental pot; rather, it is about integration that
embraces raw differences, contains distinctions and exceptions, and
defines a different whole out of this diversity.

What this whole is ultimately about remains a mystery to many.
A single European currency, a European flag, or an anthem may
hint at the emergence of a federative European superstate. Throughout history, an impressive array of thinkers and doers, from Immanuel Kant to Joschka Fischer, has advocated such a creation.
Nevertheless, the united Europe of today does not exactly resemble
a state. In fact, most attempts to build something reminiscent of a
superstate have ended in shambles.

At the same time, Europe is not a mere "regional United
Nations" either. Europe is an area of stability and prosperity and

the largest free-trade zone in the world. But it is much more than that. The EU has a parliament and an executive arm, the European Commission; it conceives the majority of the legislation to which European citizens abide in their everyday lives. The EU is an active player in world diplomacy and, increasingly, in war-torn areas around the globe. Europe does not quite resemble anything you know, but has taken bits and pieces from most of what you already have, be that a state or an international organization. It is both an actor and a process; intergovernmental and federal; laissez-faire and "dirigisme." It is a place where cultures interact and power is diluted and dispersed among myriad political, economic, social, public, and private actors. Europe is a moving target but it is still something—something utterly different.[15]

Contrary to what one might expect, all of this is not the tweedy intellectual's best-kept secret. Europe's "difference," the Europhiles muse,[16] is in the millions of travelers who ceaselessly cross the continent on low-budget airlines without needing to take their passports out of their pockets. It is in Europe's enormous and inestimable artistic heritage, as much as in the loud and wildly popular Eurovision Song Contest. Difference is in the 1.5 million students who have spent semesters in European universities through the EU's Erasmus program.

How does all of this relate to Europe's primordial opposition to the past and to its post-1989 ambitions? It does so because Europe has fulfilled its mission by having moved beyond oppositions. The European mission has become that of rising above its built-in contrasts and making its diversity Europe's gift to the world. As the French writer Albert Camus commented: "Europe has lived on its contradictions, flourished on its differences, and, constantly transcending itself thereby, has created a civilization on which the whole world depends even when rejecting it."[17]

This revolutionary constellation required a label, and several European observers have by now grown accustomed to "neo-medieval empire."[18] The term "empire" has acquired a bad reputation, to put it mildly. It evokes systems that have typically been coercive—an image that the colonial past and shameful *mission civilizatrice* of several European countries in Africa, Asia, and Latin America have, in fact, contributed to.

When applied to the European context, however, the phrase is part of a metaphor, one in which the more important word really is "neo-medieval." As in the Middle Ages, indeed, Europe is a place where power breaks down in countless players who cooperate at times and compete at others. Europe has become a multinational polity in which identities and allegiances overlap. The imperial metaphor adds the idea that borders are not rigid and static, but rather fluid and porous. It implies that power decreases the farther away one is standing from the center, which, in the case of the EU, is symbolically located in Brussels.

The metaphor also provides an intriguing angle for looking at the periphery of Europe. The periphery is where the clout of the empire is more contested and opaque, where the empire has just expanded or where it may be about to expand. It is where the neo-medieval qualities of Europe, its fuzzy borders, diffuse authority, and diluted power, are supposedly more noticeable. The periphery is where the initial correlation of security and integration meets Europe's fledgling polity. The way in which the EU has dealt with its periphery testifies to the transformation of this ambitious international actor.

THE EUROPEAN ZENITH

The EU enlargement policy has been by far the most effective tool with which Europe has dealt with its periphery. By default more than by design, enlargement has ended up becoming the archetype of the European empire. As for other empires throughout history, the expansion of the EU has filled a power vacuum in the countries in question. Like other empires, the EU has been in a position of superiority, *vis-à-vis* the countries that are candidate for membership. Nevertheless, the only way in which the imperial metaphor of Europe really resembles previous experiences of empire is, as 18th-century Russian Empress, Catherine the Great, once argued: "I have no way to defend my borders except to extend them."[19]

The enlargement of the EU has indeed embodied Europe's quest for security and stability. Sources of pressure have always brewed on the outskirts of Europe—from dictatorships on the Iberian peninsula to the communist regimes in Eastern Europe—and rendered the European integration process rather fragile. Gradual expansion toward these countries has become a basic tool in Europe's survival kit because it has essentially replicated the spirit that guided integration in Western Europe: to bind one another so tightly that waging war becomes unthinkable.

Apart from that, however, enlargement is a rather asymmetric sort of trade-off. Candidate countries adopt the so-called *acquis communautaire*, the voluminous EU rulebook now approaching some 100,000 pages of legislation, and earn their right to become part of it.

The more countries transform their institutions and rules, the closer they come to joining the EU. The clearer the EU is about what is at stake, the more a candidate country is encouraged to implement painful reforms: "governance by conditionality," to use one favorite EU term.[20]

Over the decades, the EU has rehearsed this cycle five times, in growing from the 6 original member states, into the 27-country-strong behemoth of today. Along the way, Brussels has refined and perfected this basic mechanism. As the accession of 8 former communist Central European states* in 2004 has demonstrated, Europe can claim with some pride that enlargement has become a remarkable tool for guiding the transformation of the candidate countries.

Transforming countries does not mean that Europe has worked a miracle. In the case of Central Europe, the most demanding enlargement round, the candidate countries committed to reform their judicial systems, guarantee the fundamental freedoms of their citizens, and curb corruption. They peacefully settled border disputes and agreed to treat their often troublesome minorities fairly. Aided by steady and strong growth, they have reformed their economic governance structures. In other words, they have done the work themselves.

Through the enlargement process, however, the EU did monitor their transition to liberal democracy, it guided their economic transformation, and it influenced the political culture of their societies. It is not easy to quantify success in politics. But judging by the gap in the economic and political standards separating Central Europe from their eastern cousins of the former Soviet Union, it is safe to argue that the EU has, at the very least, accompanied an extraordinary accomplishment.

What is less apparent is that this success story has deepened the "neo-medieval" features of Europe. That is so because, for one thing, the enlargement trade-off is not as uncomplicated as it seems. The progress and setbacks of the candidate countries are painstakingly monitored, benchmarked, and evaluated. This process lasts for years and involves, more or less directly, dozens of stakeholders: the governments of the candidate countries and the European institutions as well as the other EU member states, business lobbies, and civil society. Major external powers—primarily the United States, though also Russia, especially in the case of Central Europe—have

---

*Estonia, Latvia, Lithuania, Poland, Hungary, the Czech Republic, the Slovak Republic, and Slovenia, which the EU rounded up to 10 by adding the Mediterranean islands of Malta and Cyprus (or rather the southern, Greek-speaking part of the latter). In 2007, the EU also admitted Bulgaria and Romania. As I will explain in the next chapter, this latter enlargement has not turned out to be as successful as the previous one.

had an indirect stake in this venture. Enlargement is an outstanding product of Europe's polycentric polity.

Enlargement also underlines the neo-medieval traits of Europe because, as the scholar Jan Zielonka has argued, it "prevents other possible solutions from emerging."[21] The accession of new countries enriches the plurality of Europe in every field: from its governance capacity to its economic standards to foreign policy positions. New actors come to the fore, each with their own interests, strategies, and aspirations. Cultural and social identities multiply and intermingle. The more the EU enlarges, the more its diversity becomes irreversible.

Which leads to the easily misleading argument that enlargement is Europe's most successful foreign and security policy. For enlargement has undoubtedly been successful in addressing security challenges. However, candidate countries are entitled to enter the EU only once they have reformed their institutions and advanced their standards to the extent that they no longer pose any threat. Enlargement really fulfills the European mission when it *ceases* to be a foreign policy and becomes a "domestic" European matter. The key to Europe's ability to deal with external threats has been to include new countries and embrace different societies and cultures. The success of enlargement is simultaneously in Europe's power of expansion and in its power of attraction.

This is ultimately what has made of enlargement, and particularly of the landmark round involving Central Europe, one of the highest points of the European transformation. The decision to enlarge started out as the best card that Europe could put on the shaky table of post-Cold War geopolitics. As the process advanced and the candidate countries reformed, enlargement became much more. It turned into the essence of a Europe that opens up in order to spread its model of governance: a Europe willing to promote what it deems humane and "normal"[22]—from environmental protection to the abolition of the death penalty. Viewed alongside the quagmire that Washington was making for itself in Iraq, the enlargement process presented a Europe exuding confidence regarding the promise of its polity, and the scale of its ambitions.

A REALITY CHECK

The use of the past tense immediately above betrays the troubled fate for this largely unwritten manifesto. In fact, the most serious blow to the noble aspirations for Europe was dealt to the only written statement of the theory: the EU Constitutional Treaty. The initial rationale for having such a treaty was quite clear-cut. The institutions of the EU were conceived half a century ago and have adjusted as the Union took in more members but require comprehensive and more lasting reforms. A minivan built to carry 6 passengers can probably squeeze in a few more, but cannot transport more than 25 of them.

However, when the French and Dutch voters rejected the Treaty in referenda in 2005, the more ideological items of the day were the first to take the blame. According to one argument, a European "Constitution" heralds the rise of a super-state which will swallow Europe's diversity and deprive its citizens of their national identity. As center-right forces ruled throughout much of the continent, said others, the Treaty was part of a conspiracy that would sanction the ascent of a neo-liberal Europe.

Had an average voter actually studied this 300-page brick of tight legalese, it would have been quite patent that none of these claims is true. But just as no such voter ever existed, the rejection of the EU Constitution was never about the Constitution. The no vote was the sign of widespread dissatisfaction with the course of Europe. It became a way to express the growing anxiety about the future and the apprehension with multiculturalism. And it all coalesced in a largely unspecific enlargement "fatigue." Europe's insecurity became a question of its ability to take in more countries. Especially in case of the French *non*, it came down to the "Polish plumber": the imaginary new European citizen threatening the Gallic labor market with his pipes and screws. Just one year after the historic eastern expansion of the EU, the message was that the post-1989 dream of Europe had stranded.

Facts to support this gloomy mood were—and remains—all around us. For one, Europe has long been afflicted by a "culture of stagnation."[23] Large Western European economies have taken turns being labeled the "sick man of Europe." Around the time of the referendum debacle, approximately 14 million Western Europeans were unemployed—5 million in Germany alone, the highest number since the Weimar Republic. Europe has since witnessed a moderate reformist zeal in the governments of Germany and France. However, innovation continues to lag behind: Europe's universities, argued a recent study, are "slow-moving and under-funded,"[24] business is trapped in—or if necessary protected by—a jungle of red tape. The EU has espoused the bombastic goal of becoming the world's "most competitive knowledge-based economy" by 2010, but any able-minded economist will tell you that this ambition is way beyond reach.

Then came the 2008 credit turmoil and ensuing economic slump, which not only belittled the huge economic and social gains of the various Baltic and Celtic "Tigers," as well as of several former communist nations of Central Europe. Amidst the siren call of protectionism, it also seemed to put in question some of the proudest achievements of post-Wall Europe: its single market and the very reunification of the Continent.

Financial crisis notwithstanding, the demographic time bomb has never stopped ticking. Between 1990 and 2000, the number of newborns in countries such as Italy and Spain declined by about 50 percent. Eurostat, the statistical office of the EU, projects that, by 2015, deaths in Europe will, for the first time, outnumber births. By 2030, one-quarter of all Europeans will be over 65 years of age, but as life expectancy has increased, the age of retirement has fallen.[25] Besides having more babies, one obvious answer to reverse this downward trend would be immigration. Faced with Europe's exclusive labor market and with societies disinclined to cultural intermingling, however, well-educated, young migrants continue to prefer to head towards the U.S. East Coast or Silicon Valley, and Europe is left with the less educated and older migrants.

More generally, Europe is hostage of its greater or smaller idiosyncrasies—from its unnerving decision-making mechanisms to the abominable figures of its Agricultural Policy[26]—all of which are reflected in those who should benefit from the European project: the men and women in the street.

These days, the state of the public opinion about the EU is worse than opposition—it is boredom. Over the past 10 years, the level of popular attachment for the EU has never been higher than half of the European population.[27] In the member states that are traditionally skeptical regarding the EU, such as Britain, the level is predictably low. In countries such as Ireland, which have benefited enormously from European integration, the EU has long enjoyed high levels of support exceeding 65 percent; nevertheless, the Irish population proceeds to regularly reject major European treaties.[†] Europe, I have argued, is not a state, and it is fair to say that this very boredom has been instrumental in advancing complicated negotiations without the public taking note or feeling betrayed. Yet, the downside of not being fiercely opposed is that Europe is never vigorously supported.

[†]In a June 2001 referendum, the Irish people rejected the Treaty of Nice, the predecessor of the ill-fated Constitution. In June 2008, they voted against the so-called Reform Treaty, the more modest successor of the Constitution.

Europe may indeed be suffering from overstretching, but the Polish plumber cannot possibly be the cause of all this; he simply happens to be a catalyst for a broader European predicament. "Enlargement blues," a senior EU policy-maker has argued, "could be called … 'globalization blues.' The origins are much deeper in our social fabric."[28] The expansion of the EU has taken much of the heat, but the underlying—and as yet unanswered—question concerns the ability of Europe to reach to global challenges that may rapidly turn into threats. It is about what is happening outside Europe as well as inside of it. Just as the success of the EU enlargement epitomized a confident and ambitious Europe, opposition to it has become the emblem of the European crisis.

MEET THE NEIGHBORS

According to Greek mythology, when Cadmon inquired of the Oracle of Delphi the whereabouts of his kidnapped sister Europa, he received the following, frustrating clue: "You won't find her."[29]

Ask about Europe today, about its political and geographical limits, what is referred to as the "finality" of Europe, and the answer would be similarly exasperating. Is Turkey "European?" Is the Caucasus? And what about Russia? General De Gaulle, for one, famously spoke of a Europe "from the Atlantic to the Urals"—a definition that arguably comprises Turkey, the Caucasus, and Russia. The Council of Europe, the other continental organization so dear to Winston Churchill, already has an extensive membership of 47 states—including Turkey, the South Caucasian republics, and Russia. And yet, on the part of the EU, the answer as to where to find Europe has invariably proven to be ambiguous.

Some of this ambivalence is inevitable. Jostling amongst dozens of countries and stakeholders is not a recipe for straight answers. Some of it is probably deliberate. Countries wishing to enter the EU must match their words with deeds, and uncertainty is what tests their willpower and maintains their reforming impetus. The roots of this elusiveness, however, are much deeper. Elusiveness constitutes the converse of Europe's unique "difference" and the flipside of its neo-medieval polity.

Take indeed the standard "fatigue" argument. There are plenty of good reasons why the Balkan countries and Turkey would benefit from full integration in Europe. But before taking them in, the argument goes, the EU must bring its own house in order, implement the necessary institutional reforms, and take the European population with it.

This logic is plausible in the short term—as the dismal levels of public support for further enlargement suggest. It is shaky in the medium term, because in principle there are no compelling financial, budgetary or even institutional reasons preventing further EU enlargement.[30] And it crumbles miserably in the long run. The key issue is not when the EU will again be ready to expand; it is where the EU ought to end. It is not whether enlargement is Europe's most successful foreign policy; rather, it is whether the idea of taking in country after country qualifies as a foreign policy at all. Politicians may disagree on where the limits of the EU lie, but ambiguity on that hardly amounts to a strategy.

This same malaise has been conveyed into the European Neighborhood Policy. Launched in 2003, this EU policy aims at consolidating "prosperity, stability and security based on human rights, democracy and the rule of law, as well as supporting the process of reform and modernization of partners in the Union's neighborhood."[31] Initially, the EU was only meant to achieve these goals for Europe's eastern neighbors: Ukraine, Belarus, and Moldova. The idea was sensible: These countries share with the new Central European member states of the EU a communist past, an undisputable European heritage, and a common border. Moreover, these republics are, strictly speaking, the only new neighbors that the EU has acquired after the 2004 enlargement; enhancing cooperation with them would prevent the emergence of a new dividing line in the East—this time built not upon ideology but on economic and social disparities.

Nevertheless, Poland, Britain, and Sweden—the countries that called most vehemently for such a policy to be established—could not tame the powerful southern lobby within the EU. The Italians, French, and Spaniards also sought to get something out of the pre-enlargement bonanza, especially in relation to their own neighbors in North Africa and the Middle East. As a result, the current Neighborhood Policy addresses 16 partner countries,[‡] a group populated by an estimated 270 million people.

As there is little hope of bringing the former Soviet lands together with, say, Tunisia or Jordan, ambiguity was bound to show. And so it did. From the outset, the Neighborhood Policy offered "more than partnership and less than membership" to the countries neighboring Europe. All that the EU could dangle before this disparate bunch of partners was an unspecified "stake" in the European internal market. "The door," stated a top EU official, "is neither open nor shut."[32]

[‡]Morocco, Algeria, Tunisia, Libya, Egypt, Jordan, Israel, the Palestinian Authority, Lebanon, Syria, Armenia, Azerbaijan, Georgia, Moldova, Ukraine and, prospectively, Belarus.

Once again, one could spin these statements as the product of the fluid European constellation. But it is much more logical to see them as a replacement of something that the EU is no longer able to offer. It is an implicit admission that Europe is desperately attempting to reconstruct past exploits by other means. Glimpsed behind the EU's cherished diversity is cluelessness about the future of Europe.

And yet if the European periphery indeed represents an epicenter of the continent's existential dilemma, then it must also be in that same periphery, where Europe can again find itself. Is ambiguity the outcome of Europe's experimental project? Is the notion of the United Europe undergoing a mid-life crisis? Or has that notion just short-circuited? Seen from the perspective of the neighbors—and probably anybody else outside Europe—these questions are really beside the point. What matters is that the European mission started out as a direct correlation between the quest for security and that of integration. As Europe moved past that mission, it has failed to replace it with something equally sensible.

Instead, Europe has seemingly unlearned its former skills and reverted to pursuing security by closing up and keeping threats at a distance. It either emphasizes security by trying to hold external challenges out or it focuses on integration by debating endlessly alternative combinations of deeper cooperation among the existing member countries. It appears as though the basic condition for the EU to exist is as an environment sterilized of any threat that might prevent deeper integration. The paradox here is that post-war Europe emerged amid the rubble of war, tyranny, and poverty and in a geopolitical environment teeming with threats. In terms of dealing the neighbors, Europe may have overcome its past, but it has also cut off its roots.

At a time when Europe's post-Wall ambitions are in the doldrums, Europe again requires something in which it can look at itself: something that neither deforms nor magnifies its image. It needs a mirror that provides an objective sense of what Europe is and what it is capable of. It needs again an opposite, which presents challenges or even threats, something that is both distinct and indissolubly bound to Europe.

The countries neighboring Europe are the most obvious candidates for this task. Each in its own way, these countries challenge the distinctive achievements of Europe. Criminality and corruption or human rights violations defy the European belief in the transformative power of law. Immigration is perceived as a threat to the European welfare state and to the stability of its society as a whole.

The Turkish EU bid is seen as a challenge to the European secular modernity. Many of the countries in this region are ravaged by ethno-nationalist conflicts and are under the oppression of autocracies, and extreme poverty remains a plague. The very same constitutive challenges that made contemporary Europe are coalescing in the European periphery. This realization elicits apprehension and ultimately rejection. But it is also a humbling reminder that Europe needs not continually reinvent itself. Its original mission is far from accomplished and remains very close to home.

2

The Path to Normalcy

In Sarajevo, you have it all within a mile. On the one end, stands the pockmarked "Marshall Tito" barracks, now part of the university and thronging with natural scientists in their immaculate white lab coats. On the other end, towers the heavily guarded headquarters of the High Representative in Bosnia and Herzegovina. In between runs one of the city's main boulevards, infamous in the early 1990s as "Sniper Alley," and where today a dozen rusting police Volkswagens sleepily observe the traffic streaming in and out of town.

Regrettably, there are other, more revealing places testifying to the rough path of the Balkan countries towards a resumption of what might be called normalcy. The High Representative is not the only figure deployed by the international community to keep the peace and build the states in the region. The barracks-turned-university may not be the most impressive spot to document the rebirth of Sarajevo either; that would have to be the enchanted old town, which once thrived in its ethnic diversity and now struggles to show the world that "what Europe wants to be, Bosnia has already been."[1]

Nevertheless, it is in that potholed mile—and in that fleet of police cars in the middle of it—where the atavistic feuds of the Balkans finally reconcile with the timid steps taken by the region towards Europe. Or, at least, that is how Brussels likes to look at it. The EU hailed a long-awaited—and still shaky—deal in 2008 about the Bosnian police force as one of the successes of the European strategy in the region. The agreement was to demonstrate the willingness of the country's different factions to move beyond ethnic partisanship and steer their institutions towards a fully self-sustaining outcome.

Some may understandably dismiss this reading as a familiar European overreaction: Europeans persevere with their excitement about negotiations and rules, while the Balkans, from combustible interethnic relations to the rhetoric of local politicians, remains a tinderbox. But there is more here than meets the eye.

The Balkans* is the one place in the European periphery where everything coalesces. From its nascent common defense policy to the enlargement process, this is the region where Europe's basic nexus of security and integration can be best replicated. If progress in a relatively obscure matter such as police reform is heralded as an historic achievement, it is not necessarily out of cynicism or a badly concealed sense of guilt. Rather, it is because, in the Balkans, most of what the EU has been working to achieve beyond its borders is on the line.

BARBARIANS NO MORE?

"This," wrote the last U.S. ambassador to Yugoslavia, "is a story with villains."[2] Those who followed the Yugoslavian breakup can probably agree with this assessment. But challenge them to place these villains, give them a name, or set a timeframe to their exploits and that consensus typically vanishes.

The first usual suspects are the region's real or alleged butchers, responding to the names of Milosevic, Tudjman, or Karadzic—depending on whom you talk to. A bellicose minority in the region continues to blame foreign conspiracies, cooked up by—depending, again, on the interlocutor—the United States, Germany, or even the Vatican. Just as divisive an exercise is to pin down when the villains actually began operating, with the options ranging from 1991 all the way back to the 14th century.

This exhausting blame game has been going on for years. A seemingly uncontroversial way around it for Western observers has been to trace it all back to the region's congenital hatred, primitive violence, and backwardness. According to this argument, it all went wrong when the Balkans' "monopoly of barbarity"[3] metastasized into aggressive nationalism. We "lost" the Balkans, commentators unimaginatively put it, when the degenerate chauvinism of the few manipulated the mind of the many into the myth of a Greater Serbia, Greater Croatia, or Greater Albania.

That cannot possibly be the only interpretation of the atrocities that followed, but it is one that has ostensibly made better sense in

---

*Here I will look at what the EU calls the "Western Balkans": Croatia, Macedonia (formally known as the Former Yugoslav Republic of Macedonia), Albania, Montenegro, Serbia, Bosnia and Herzegovina, and Kosovo.

the Western imagination.[4] Over 100,000 deaths, half of the Bosnian population driven from their homes, the 30 pounds of weight that the average Bosnian lost during the war—have given all of the proof to single out the Balkan barbarity.

This line of reasoning has certainly matched well with Europe, where a standard diagnosis has been that nationalism is the Balkans' most deadly poison. The region will meet its "European future" (another familiarly unimaginative catchphrase) once its corrosive nationalist instincts will have been absorbed into the European framework. The transformation is gradual and can materialize in different guises: from the electoral successes of reformist forces in Serbia to the endurance of Macedonia's constitutional setup to, indeed, the Bosnian police reform. Whenever one or all of these things happens, European leaders can be heard breathing a sigh of relief or, worse, trumpeting the virtues of the European gospel.[5]

Rather than bringing us closer to the sources of the Balkan conundrum, however, this characterization distorts some facts on the ground. Europe's record on nationalism, for one, is not so straight. For all of the enthused emphasis on shared sovereignty, Europe has not really consigned nationalism to the history books. European nationalism has no doubt matured, but it has not entirely been tamed by the EU—the independentist claims within Spain or Belgium's wafer-thin federalism testifying to its resilience.

Add to that Europe's own experience with "ethnic disaggregation." After 1945, some 7 million Germans were driven out of non-German countries in Central Europe, 1.5 million Poles living in the Soviet Union were sent back to Poland, and most of the Jews that were left in Europe fled to the United States and Israel. Contemporary Europe may well be post-national. But as scholar Jerry Z. Muller has astutely noted, that is because this methodical "ethnic unmixing" has emptied nationalism of its more degenerative and viral aspects. The violent disintegration of Yugoslavia—with its appalling coda of ethnic cleansing—may well be regarded as "the last act of a long play."[6]

Second, there is the record of nationalism itself. In light of the profound existential dilemmas that continue to bedevil the region, ethnic nationalism has given its very worst in the Balkans. At the same time, this stigma has not quite shaken the more positive views regarding the role of nationalism in the modernization of societies.

Nationalism remains the one bond that has enabled the emergence of more solidaristic, law-abiding, and even prosperous communities. It is the glue of the modern citizenry because, as British thinker Ernest Gellner has argued, it summons two of society's most basic needs: its ability to produce and the ability to defend itself.[7] The same cannot be said of—to recall another typical Balkan marker—tribalism, which traditionally emerged in volatile environments where self-defense is a higher priority than development.

Granted, nationalism in democratizing states has, more often than not, proven to be a source of instability. And yes, nations overlap linguistically, religiously, and territorially to such an extent that it is inconceivable to imagine that every nation can or should produce a state. Still, this stark contrast between good European transformation and bad Balkan nationalism is misleading, in so far as it polarizes Europe and the Balkans as two clashing and irreconcilable forces.

Replace nationalism with criminality, and Europe's Balkan nightmare begins to show its true face. The region's desolate landscape of cronyism, clientelism, and corrupt policing is all but new. It would be tempting to relapse into the argument concerning the Balkans' savage banditism, its gun-loving history, and the role played by both in the formation of these states. In the Balkans, the argument forwarded by sociologist Charles Tilly that state-making is really organized crime at the highest level,[8] is not as exotic as it sounds.

As opposed to the disquisitions on nationalism, however, Europe's main worry is not about the historical origins of Balkan criminality. As one dark joke goes, the concern is that while some states have mafias, the Balkan mafia has got the state. European policy-makers have long been concerned by the security apparatus in Serbia, for its legacy of war crimes, but also for its involvement in the more mundane practices of abduction, extortion, and trafficking. They nervously keep an eye on Bosnia and Kosovo as well as the ways in which organized crime has filled the gaps left unattended by state and international institutions there. Then there are the region's unemployment rates (in Kosovo and Bosnia, somewhere around 40 percent) and the striking poverty of some of its parts (per capita annual income in Kosovo is estimated at around $1,800). Europeans do not need to have read their Tilly in order to fear a basic association between poverty and unemployment on the one hand, and the potential appeal of criminality on the other.

Even more distressing are the ways and extent to which this lawlessness is intertwined with Europe itself. The concerns of Europeans become tangible when they get to learn that, in recent years, almost half of the heroin seizures in Germany have been made on the country's southern border, or that Albanians control some 80 percent of the Swiss heroin market. Europeans worry when they realize that among the more than 2 million people who have fled the Balkans in the past decade to reach Germany, Italy, or the Nordic countries, thousands have fallen victim to the net of traffickers. During the wars in the 1990s, a forte of some of the regimes and their wandering paramilitaries was also the arms trade. Weapons trafficking receives comparably limited attention today, although one concern is that those arms would come in handy to terrorists of various sorts, including those of an Islamist persuasion.[9]

Also here, however, Europe shares much more than it cares to admit with the Balkans. That is surely because the Balkan gangland, as elsewhere, has gone global. Crime syndicates have laundered cash and reputation in legitimate businesses and in joint ventures together with their European peers. However, this alone cannot explain why Croatia ranks better on the Transparency International Corruption Perception Index than Romania and Bulgaria, two EU member states. Or why, according to a United Nations survey, the recorded crime rates of EU member Greece and those of Macedonia are essentially the same.[10] The story of Milorad Milakovic, a notorious sex trafficker, made it into the pages of the *National Geographic* also because he used to live in a castle in northwest Bosnia, surrounded by his bodyguards and three Siberian tigers. But the disheartened Balkan observer would have every right to wonder: How is that different from the Italian underworld boss who had his immense Naples mansion modeled to the last detail on that of Tony Montana of Hollywood's classic *Scarface*?[11]

The region's vicinity has evidently hurt the pride of Europe, amplified its outrage, and exacerbated its instinctive rejection of the Balkans. Yet vicinity is also a fastidious reminder that the Balkans is both deeply embedded to the European past and not too far from its present.

A TWO-STORY BUILDING

In foreign policy parlance, "nation-building" is the label of choice to describe the job, often performed with the decisive contribution of foreign powers, of weaving the economic, political, and security fabric of a society emerging from conflict. From Germany and Japan after 1945 to Afghanistan and Iraq in this decade, nation-building has involved a variety of tasks: humanitarian relief, post-conflict reconstruction, the restructuring of institutions, and everything in between.[12]

In light of all that the Balkans went through in the name of nationalism, the term "nation-building" in itself may sound some-what inauspicious. In any case, Europeans have felt the need to do things differently in this region, in a way that has been dubbed: "member state–building."[13]

The phrase reveals two tiers. One ("state") largely coincides with what is understood as nation-building. The other ("member") does not diverge fundamentally from the standard approach that led the former communist countries of Central Europe into the EU. But it is when taken together that member state–building becomes an unprecedented approach.

Europe has steered the "state" part of the strategy with the other foreign and international actors operating in the Balkans, and has been backed by substantial investments. With the necessary adjustments, per capita economic assistance to Bosnia in the two post-war years was five times greater than that given to Germany in the same time-span after World War II. As of 2005, the figure for Kosovo was some 25 times higher than what had been poured into Afghanistan since the 2002 intervention toppled the Taliban. The latter comparison probably says more about the means allocated to the Afghan reconstruction than about Kosovo. Still, the economic and political capital invested in the Balkans has been massive. And Europeans have contributed the biggest share of it.[14]

The EU flag is, at last, also visible on the sleeves of European soldiers. The EU has deployed some 10,000 personnel in seven different missions in Bosnia, Macedonia, and, most recently, independent Kosovo. These have included some of the most wide-ranging operations in which the EU has embarked under its embryonic defense policy. European boots have been engaged in duties as diverse as traditional peacekeeping and police assistance.

That defense policy has never been a European asset is an understatement. So it is hardly surprising that the present operations have encountered a number of difficulties as regards the coordination between their civilian and military components and the various EU agencies. Moreover, the security of the local population should logically figure among the very first priorities on the state-building scale, but the EU has only managed to deploy its relatively puny firepower since 2003. Still, the conditions on the ground have fortunately improved. Compared to the impotence of the thousands of white-clad monitors deployed in the 1990s (the "ice cream men," went another dark joke), peace is, for better or worse, being kept.

Europe has also gotten involved in the constitutions of the Balkan countries. The EU intervened, this time in a timelier manner, in

2001, in the negotiations in Macedonia. The ensuing multi-ethnic arrangement, guaranteeing rights to the country's significant Albanian minority, is probably the only one that can be said to be working in the Balkans at the moment. Brussels had pushed for a loose state union of Serbia and Montenegro, before resigning to Montenegro's peaceful secession from Serbia in 2006. The EU is striving to move beyond the international protectorate in Bosnia—still the one brokered by the United States in Dayton in 1995.

The reason why Europe's hand has been heavy on the constitutional arrangements is connected to the "member" part of the strategy. Since 1999, the Balkans has been part of something called the Stabilization and Association Process, a stage midway on the path towards EU membership. Strictly speaking, these countries are not in the same boat in this matter: Croatia might be ready to join the EU as soon as 2011; Serbia and Bosnia first signed a halfway agreement with Brussels only in 2008. But in all cases, this process has been about pointing every element of the respective transitions of these countries—including their constitutional setup—in the direction of Europe.

What does bring these countries together is the crucial extra demand to cooperate with each other. Inevitably, regional cooperation sends bad vibrations throughout the Balkans; many in the region even fear that the international community is plotting a subtle reconstitution of the Yugoslav federation. But after the bloodshed of the 1990s, this request is fairly intuitive. Before entering Europe, the Balkans must demonstrate a basic ability to move beyond wary coexistence. Even more intuitively, regionalism is meant to replicate the very rationale of European integration on a smaller scale.[15] After 1999, the international community had to impose regional cooperation upon the reluctant Balkans. The task now becomes how to get the Balkan nations to steer the regional process by themselves.

Stability and Association, "state" and "member": Europe's Balkan strategy faithfully resembles the well-rehearsed EU enlargement process, its rigorous mechanism of conditions and incentives, and that painstaking correlation of security and integration priorities applied in Central Europe. There is a crucial difference, however. For any of the Central European countries, the task of reforming the state and approaching EU membership proceeded largely in parallel. The more economic and political transformation progressed, the juicier the European enlargement carrot became.

For the Balkans, the exercise of stabilization and association is sequential rather than synchronic. Once the Balkan countries have demonstrated that they have the basic pillars of their institutions in place, they are entitled to approach their European future. Europe needs to make sure that they have stabilized, before they can associate. Stated differently, what separates "member" from "state-" building is a rather steep ladder that the Balkan governments and their peoples have to climb. Each nation-building deed is not just nation-building, but a stock option regarding the future participation of these countries in the EU.[16]

This shift is sensitive, and the task as a whole is monumental, but after the economic and social breakdown inherited from the 1990s, the member-state sequencing appears perfectly logical. The progression on that ladder is as painstaking as it is almost imperceptible. The Balkans rarely makes the headlines anymore. And that is precisely the point at which the building of Europe's Balkan policy begins to creak.

WHAT THEY OWN . . .

Most strategists will strongly advise against declaring "mission accomplished" once an international force has concluded major combat operations in a troubled country. They will argue that internationals must continue to play a role in the medium to long term in order to ensure that the transition proceeds in a secure environment. In fact, internationals often ensure that the transition happens in the first place.

Sooner rather than later, however, once the mission is indeed largely deemed accomplished, policy-makers are confronted with a number of tough questions: To what extent can locals take charge of their own affairs? How should internationals transfer power? And, above all, when will locals truly "own" their country?

The "ownership" question has stirred an intense debate in relation to the Balkans, with at least two distinct schools of thought. The first camp contends that it is unjustified that foreign administrators, such as the High Representative in Bosnia, have held the power for so long to impose laws, create institutions, and fire local officials. It is unsustainable for internationals to act like a colonial "Raj." The time has now come to shift gear; internationals must step back and locals must take responsibility.[17]

The second school believes that if these nations have not yet taken charge of their own business, it is because they are incapable of doing so. When war breaks every channel of civilized interaction, it is unrealistic to believe that a modus of peaceful relations is going to be re-established by simply handing back the reins to locals. The international presence in the Balkans must change. But ownership cannot be the tool to achieve that change; it must be the end result.

Kosovo's independence from Serbia, declared in February 2008, provides a recent illustration of this dilemma. The mantra guiding this issue was that the independence aspirations of Kosovo Albanians might have been illegal from a formal standpoint, but were legitimate from a substantial and humanitarian perspective. Having suffered persecution at the hand of Milosevic's Serbia, followed by an increasingly dysfunctional UN administration for nine years, the Kosovars deserved their freedom.

The Serbs went as far as suggesting for Kosovo an arrangement similar to that between Hong Kong and China. But even that kind of autonomy, like all of the other proposals that have been floated over the past decade, proved inadequate for somebody who takes independence as the only answer. By necessity—and regardless of what people in Belgrade and Russia (staunchly supporting the Serbs) might still argue—Western policy has construed the Kosovo case as unique.

Even so, the solution that has finally been implemented is a paradigmatic outcome of the perils of the international presence in post-conflict societies. Kosovo could not turn into another Bosnia, continuing the decade-long UN protectorate there by other means. But it was not deemed ready for a Macedonian solution, which would have meant a fully sovereign state in Kosovo based on a multi-ethnic arrangement between the overwhelming majority of Albanians and the Serbian minority.

The international community—or, rather, the Western countries—eventually resolved that the right mix was somewhere between the Bosnian and Macedonian recipes. The new Republic in Pristina does not have the divisive traits of Bosnia's setup and is committed to the protection and representation of the country's Serb minority. The EU "supervises" (read, oversees key government functions) Kosovo's path to full sovereignty with a couple thousands of its men. However, Kosovo today hangs in limbo, its sovereignty recognized by neither Serbia nor the UN nor, more awkwardly, by all EU member states (the supposed "supervisors").

The bottom line is that there is no silver bullet for the ownership dilemma. The Macedonian experience, for example, is sometimes vaunted as a European success story because the government in Skopje has demonstrated a basic ability to steer its own institutions. However, entrenched inter-ethnic divisions and occasional bursts of violence testify to the country's continued volatility.

In contrast, an international protectorate is never going to make a very convincing case about ownership. And yet Bosnia regressed to a hazardous stalemate precisely when, in 2006–2007, internationals had resolved that it was time to hand power back to the Bosnians. As Bosnia descended into vicious political infighting, the High Representative was back to sharpening the yardsticks that ought to enable him at some point to pass the baton to the EU and then, hopefully, to the Bosnians themselves.[18]

The issues of how, when, and to what extent power should be handed back are bound to remain extremely sensitive for the international community. For locals, these issues remain exasperatingly hazy.

... AND WHAT THEY GET

This uncertainty is mirrored by the set of incentives and penalties that is meant to guide these countries towards Europe. Rational considerations are supposed to be behind this process, namely, the expectation that a Balkan country fulfills European demands because it perceives them as necessary for its own development. A more abstract—almost romantic—rationale validates the European requests on higher moral grounds of democracy and justice. Somehow bridging these two motivations is the sort of virtuous cycle by which countries develop a sense of belonging to the broader European community as they abide to its norms and rules.

The problem is that as soon as the cycle loses its rigor, the whole mechanism loses some of its logic. The case in point here is the role played by the International Criminal Tribunal for the former Yugoslavia. Since its inception in the early 1990s, the Tribunal, based in The Hague, has slowly emerged as one of the key institutions for some of these countries. Sociologists have disputed whether justice for the victims of some of the most heinous crimes favors or undermines the quest for the reconciliation of war-scarred communities. Many in Serbia, for instance, still regard the Tribunal as a diabolical instrument created to humiliate their nation. This notwithstanding, full cooperation with The Hague has been identified as one of the crucial conditions to be met by the countries involved in the Yugoslav war when approaching EU membership.

Yet, the meaning of "full cooperation" has been dangerously in flux over the years. By the autumn of 2005, for example, Croatia had failed to secure the arrest of General Ante Gotovina, its main wartime fugitive. That was a deficiency that Carla Del Ponte, then-Chief

Prosecutor of the Hague Tribunal, had made sure to underline, and it should have prevented Zagreb from opening accession negotiations with the EU. Yet, with Austria dragging its feet to defend Croatia, its old Habsburg relative, the EU was forced to call on the otherwise combative Del Ponte to certify with some syntactic acrobatics that Zagreb was, well, cooperating with the Tribunal, after all. Gotovina was arrested a couple of months later, but accession negotiations with Croatia started in October 2005, as the General was conspicuously absent.

Serbia has followed a similar—if more tormented—trajectory. In May 2006, Brussels suspended talks on its midway agreement with Belgrade because Serbia had failed to cooperate with the Tribunal on the arrests and transfers of its main suspects—including Bosnian Serb leaders, Ratko Mladic and Radovan Karadzic. Since then, stability in and around Serbia has been balanced on a tightrope: Montenegro seceded, Kosovo declared its independence, and radicals remained a firm reference point for almost half of the Serbian population. The EU felt it necessary to loosen its grip on the issue of cooperation with the Tribunal to support pro-European forces. The midway deal with Serbia was signed (but not ratified) in April 2008, as the main fugitives remained at large. And as in Gotovina's case, Karadzic was finally arrested in July 2008.

Whether or not this ambivalence regarding cooperation with the Court has had some impact on the reconciliation process in the Balkans may be impossible to measure. Nonetheless, the examples about the Croatian and Serbian cooperation with The Hague are microcosms illustrating the fragilities of the European strategy in this region. Some room for maneuvering and even brinkmanship when dealing with problematic countries is nothing new and has its benefits. Indeed, the offer of a pre-accession agreement to Serbia, the 2008 electoral victory of pro-EU forces in that country, and the subsequent arrest of Karadzic is not a coincidental chain of events. It demonstrates the advantages of calibrating moves according to the situation on the ground. However, for a strategy based primarily on setting and implementing rules—such as the one pursued by the EU—bending rules risks undermining the strategy as a whole. If the strict European conditions are perceived as relative or, worse, arbitrary, domestic reforms run the risk of stalling or, worse, reversing. This ambivalence may lead partner countries to believe that they can get away with almost anything, only to redeem themselves when the going gets too tough.

It is a difficult balance, no doubt. And when the process is so slow and the spotlight elsewhere, a weakening of the European strategy may be difficult to discern. As opposed to reconciliation, however, this weakness can somehow be measured.

THE MEASURE OF CREDIBILITY

It must be because he is at ease with quoting philosophers of the Enlightenment; it could be because he was educated in the United States; or maybe it is because, by definition, he is expected to be a wise man. Whatever the reason, when Mustafa Ceric, the highest religious authority for the Muslim population in Bosnia, refers to the "social contract"[19] to describe what Europe is all about, one wonders whether the job of bringing the Balkans into the EU can be so difficult after all.

Europe's engagement in the region is meant to represent a sort of social contract writ large. As for other types of contracts, the parties have stipulated a set of rights and obligations. The "social" aspect of it relates to the consent to delegate certain state prerogatives to the EU. As in other contracts, however, some items in small print have raised serious issues regarding interpretation.

The need among the Balkan countries to overcome their past and secure their European future is a no-brainer. Europe has taken serious political and economic strides, and it has backed these deeds with an innovative approach. But singling out the Balkans as the last European aberration has not helped to catalyze these resources. This posture has contributed to perpetuating the region's existential quandary and, in the process it has ended up entangling Europe's own capabilities. The European instinct to reject the Balkans concerns the enormous challenges facing the region no less than it concerns Europe's ruminations about its own future. In both instances, the result has been an ambivalent interpretation of the scrupulous EU metrics and an erosion of Europe's credibility.

Europe faces some stiff competition on the credibility question. The United States may not "have a dog" in the Balkans fight—as former Secretary of State James Baker already argued during the war in the 1990s. However, Washington's political and diplomatic engagement is still highly valued in Bosnia, Albania, and Kosovo, while NATO membership is a more tangible prospect for some of the countries in the region.[20] Russia is also putting its money where its mouth is, with economic investments in key strategic assets of Serbia and of the Srpska Republic, the Bosnian Serb entity populated by ethnic Serbs.

Europe is flexing much greater military and economic muscle than either the United States or Russia. It possesses the means to coerce and has learned to exercise it. Its ability to deliver, however, rests primarily on the sanctity of its contract with the Balkan countries. Its execution is a voluntary affair and places the burden of the regional transition on the Balkan countries as much as on Europe itself.

What renders the European strategy groundbreaking is that political will must come from Europe as much as from the countries concerned. That, however, is also what makes the approach more costly and more fragile. It only takes two contrasting official statements for mighty Europe to find itself in the awkward position of having to reassure the Balkan capitals concerning its commitment to the region.[21] In light of the indefensible blunders made in the 1990s, a certain fixation with credibility is unavoidable, and even welcome. But the more Europeans feel the need to reiterate their consistency, the less the disenchanted peoples in the Balkans will tend to believe them.

Many in Europe and the region have argued that one solution to this would be to indicate a tentative date of accession of the Balkan countries in the EU. Some have claimed that the year 2014 would be a feasible deadline for the entire region to enter the Union. It would be symbolically powerful, too, solemnly marking the end of a bloody century that had started in 1914 with the assassination of Archduke Franz Ferdinand in Sarajevo.[22]

The truth is, that when it comes to deadlines, the EU has been there already. Brussels gave Romania and Bulgaria, the two more advanced Balkan countries, a deadline for their entry into the EU. Since their accession in 2007, painful judicial and administrative reforms have slowed down, and these countries continue to struggle against contract killings and corruption. Giving Bulgaria and Romania that EU membership date was equivalent to awarding a Master's degree to a university freshman—and then assuming that the student will continue studying.

Ultimately, the diatribes over a tentative date of accession are no different from the disagreements over a more or less lenient attitude toward The Hague Tribunal or the various experiments on "ownership." As important as they all may be, none of these debates really sends a concrete signal about the proclaimed desire to have the Balkans in the EU.

That signal must come from elsewhere: the prospect for the Balkan people to travel freely in Europe, the opportunity for companies to trade and invest more easily, or for more Balkan students to spend a semester in European universities.[23] If these actions are approached as a tick-the-box exercise, they will remain merely technical measures. If they are superseded by discussions over the limits of EU enlargement, they will become lost in Europe's internal squabbles. But with unequivocal political and financial backing, the impact of these kinds of targeted measures is priceless. The European strategy makes a difference when its firm conditions deliver concrete benefits to the Balkan citizens. That, in the last instance, is the only measure of Europe's credibility.

3

Turkish Ironies

"The enlargement process is on track—not a bullet train, but on track," "like the Orient Express," "no TGV [Train à Grande Vitesse]."[1] The European Commission clearly likes train metaphors. And rightly so. The image is spot on for capturing the gradualism and resilience of the negotiations regarding the accession of Turkey to the EU. It probably also adds a somewhat evocative touch to an exercise so protracted and—let it be said—dull, as the enlargement.

In recent years, however, Turkey has been shaken to its core by profound political and societal turmoil. Europeans continue to worry about their labor market stability, cultural identity, and the economic assistance that will be necessary to feed the Turkish EU ambitions. The enlargement process has noticeably slowed down, and the European Commission has returned to the image in order to visualize the specter of a head-on confrontation: The EU and Turkey, Ankara has been warned, might be heading for a "train crash."

It is revealing that the train metaphor is being used to describe the same country and the same matter but with the purpose of conveying two opposite messages: that the expansion of the EU is meant to be an entirely predictable, almost deterministic phenomenon, but that the EU and Turkey are possibly on a collision course. The enigma of the EU-Turkey relations is all there—in a series of contradictions beginning with the country's contested identity and ending in the geostrategic future of Europe. In those contradictions are the roots of the disagreement and of the mutual disenchantment, and there are also hidden some unlikely glimmers of hope in Europe's Turkey dilemma.

THE MOST MODERN OF THEM ALL

The excerpt is rather long and not particularly reader-friendly, but the following words of the Turkish Armed Forces are worth a read:

> In the last days, the issue that came to the foreground during the presidential elections was focused on debating secularity. This situation is being observed with concern by the Turkish Armed Forces. It should not be forgotten that the Turkish Armed Forces are a side in this debate and are a staunch defender of secularism. Moreover, it should not be forgotten that the Turkish Armed Forces are absolutely against the discussions and negative interpretations, and that it will clearly and openly display its position and attitudes when it becomes necessary. No one should doubt that.[2]

This is part of a "memorandum" issued by the Turkish General Staff in April 2007 in response to the candidature of ex-Islamist Foreign Minister, Abdullah Gül to the Presidency of the Republic. In July of that year, following a ruling by the Constitutional Court and mass protests, the majority Justice and Development Party (AKP, by its Turkish acronym), to which Gül belonged, called for a snap election, which it won by a landslide. This lent legitimacy to the bid made by the Foreign Minister, who was subsequently elected President.

This ostensibly happy ending does not detract from the significance of the event. That is, for one, because the powerful Turkish top brass usually walks the walk ("no one should doubt that") and has felt compelled to intervene in the country's civilian institutions on no less than four occasions since 1960. Instead, this statement will go down as the first "*e*-coup" in history: It was posted on the General Staff website, and its warnings have remained confined to cyberspace. Moreover, the incident is important because the issue of secularism, upon which the message was centered, has long held a firm place in the soul of modern Turkey.

Contemporary Turkey remains the most venerated legacy of Mustafa Kemal (better known as "Atatürk"), his revolution, and his monumental state-building enterprise. After the end of World War I, Atatürk set about to reshape the dismembered community he had inherited from the Ottoman Empire. He did so by attributing a central role to the state in governing the Turkish economic structures. He introduced populism, which, by his standards concerned the sidelining of class and ethnic divisions within society. Atatürk aimed uncompromisingly for Western modernity, which he pursued by inventing, codifying, and implementing "Turkishness."[3]

The relationship between religion and politics in Turkey has not constituted the only quandary confronting this colossal venture. Center vs. periphery, urban vs. rural, ethnic diversity vs. cultural homogeneity: Atatürk embarked upon a project of social engineering the magnitude of which has busied the rulers of Turkey for decades and on multiple fronts. Possibly the most formidable challenge of all, however, was that Atatürk succeeded in forging a modern state without a modern nation developing in its wake. In that respect, transforming Islam from an organizing societal principle into an individualistic belief—a belief, it should be recalled, that is shared by 99 percent of Turkey's 71 million citizens—was bound to prove a particularly bitter bone of contention.

Throughout the troubled history of modern Turkey, political Islam and the so-called "Kemalist" establishment—which includes the military—have crossed paths repeatedly. In order to prevent Islamization, the secular elite has not hesitated to shut down Islamist parties. Even the current Prime Minister, Recep Tayyip Erdogan, was once incarcerated for reciting verses from an Islamic poem in public. At the same time, when challenged by emerging leftist movements in the 1960s and 1970s, the Kemalists actually boosted Islamism and disenfranchised it as a legitimate social and political force.

In spite of such a hectic past, the first resounding victory for the AKP in the general elections of 2002 still represented a political earthquake. Having shelved the radical rhetoric of previous Islamist outfits, the AKP shifted towards more centrist positions. The platform reached out to the core constituency of the party in the pious Anatolian heartland. Furthermore, it appealed to the urban middle class, the business community, and anyone who had grown embittered with the exclusionary narrative of the secular establishment. The electoral masterpiece of the AKP was to brand a party with roots in political Islam as the champion of a more modern Turkey.

Precisely in this move, however, lay the seeds of confrontation. The highest eschelons of traditional Turkey still regard themselves— and Atatürk's heritage they preserve—as the depository of Turkish modernity. The AKP may be a self-styled version of the German Christian Democrats, a social conservative and moderately religious party. For some secularists, however, any relaxation of Atatürk's precepts represents a potential threat to the stability of the country or, as Yasar Büyükanit, a former top general, put it, "crafty plans" aimed at destroying "the gains of modernity."[4]

On balance, the record of the Erdogan government is hardly suggestive of a fundamentalist agenda. Even so, serious tactical blunders have been made. The AKP sought to outlaw adultery before ultimately deciding against doing so. Alcohol-free zones popped up in some of the smaller cities. After the 2007 presidential election saga, the government repealed the ban on headscarves in public universities, one of the cherished symbols of secularism. In 2008, the latter move led to a dramatic case in the Constitutional Court in which the AKP stood accused of imposing Sharia law, which it only narrowly survived.

Unsurprisingly, this series of occurrences has been anything but beneficial to the Turkish quest for modernity. The debate has fallen prey to ideologues and has fanned the flames of chauvinism on both sides.[5] A less obvious side effect is how Europe and the EU have become embroiled in this spiral. Westernization has always been at the heart of the Kemalist vision of modernization, and the Turkish secular intelligentsia has historically been pro-Europe as a result. The irony here is that Turkey has never come so close to experiencing the intrusive side of Europeanization since the AKP has come to power. So, for some segments of the traditional establishment, the EU has turned from a powerful agent of modernization into a symbol of decadence and a threat to the foundations of the Turkish state.

There have been sufficient instances in recent years for those wishing to make this case. Any measure strengthening the civilian oversight of the military can easily be branded as a usurpation of national sovereignty. Reforms encouraging multiculturalism can foment tensions with Turkey's sizeable Kurdish minority. By pressing the government to repeal the controversial article 301 of the Penal Code—which made it illegal to insult "Turkishness"—Brussels essentially claimed competences belonging to the state. The government's Euro-fervor has become the strongest indictment against the AKP, and Europeanization has come to represent the Trojan horse aiming at the country's political system. The elements of the secular elite that were formerly at the forefront of the modernization of Turkey have become more introverted, insular, and Euro-skeptical.

The final twist is that the European posture toward Turkey has itself become increasingly introverted and insular. The European project, I have argued, concerns the encounter of competing ways of interpreting its core values. The rights of ethnic minorities have been arranged differently in European countries, as have the civil–military relations. Europe is about both the more liberal blend of secularism as well as the stricter *laïcité*. The European modernity is supposedly about diversity and inclusion, rounding off edges rather than sharpening them. Europe is "post-modern," precisely because it rejects absolute and univocal explanations of what "modern" is supposed to mean.

Yet, in relation to Turkey the canons defining European modernity have become inflexible and non-negotiable. Turkey is supposed to be aiming for European-style modernity—whatever that is. Should Ankara turn away from the EU rules and conditions, its European journey will suffer. More than that, however, the encrypted message is that Turkey will have chosen to reject modernity.

TECHNOCRACY AND ITS PERILS

The story has been going on for half a century. Turkey first applied to become an associated member of the then European Economic Community in 1959, a goal it attained in 1963. Ankara subsequently applied for full membership in 1987. The EU officially recognized Turkey as a candidate country in 1999 and opened accession talks with Ankara in 2005.

This last leg in particular, the formalization of an EU perspective, has tremendously influenced Turkey's legal, social, and economic landscape. Judicial reforms have attained notable results. The rights of women and minorities have been strengthened, the death penalty has been abolished, the penal code reformed. Despite its massive regional disparities, the record of the Turkish economy has also improved greatly. With the support of the International Monetary Fund, Turkey has managed to stabilize fiscal and monetary policies. The inflation rate has fallen, and until 2008 the GDP has been growing at a steady 7.5 percent annually since the AKP came to power—"Islamic Calvinists," hailed one report.[6]

As in the case of Central European countries, the architects of this feat are to be found within Turkey itself, not in Brussels. Yet, according to the European vulgate, this outstanding transformation contains all of the ingredients of the methods and practices of the EU. The EU has proven an important anchor to reform because of its strict conditions and its unwavering rigor. Were it not for the stimulus, pressure, and support coming from Brussels, Turkey may have not embarked in such overarching changes, or, at the very least, it would have done so more slowly. The directions of Ankara's reforms as well as the experience of previous expansions, provide plenty of evidence to argue that Turkey has transformed also thanks to the EU.

More than any other EU candidate, however, the case of Turkey underscores what is possibly the most serious fallacy of the EU enlargement rhetoric. The European language very strongly conveys the impression that the expansion of the EU is a neutral and objective process and based on the strict application of the rules. The EU drafted a feasibility report before giving Turkey its go-ahead. It publishes annual progress reports. The EU monitors and evaluates developments and ponders decisions on that basis. It would appear as though the Turkey dossier is in the safe hands of a bespectacled surgeon.

As policy-makers in Europe and Turkey well know, however, the EU enlargement is not merely a *technical*, but also an eminently *political* exercise. Benchmarks and figures are important and highly regarded; however, they are often the starting point for squabbles among European countries and stakeholders. These discussions often have very little to do with the allegedly technical nature of enlargement or, for that matter, with enlargement itself. As Turkey scholar Nathalie Tocci has noted, they "largely act as proxies for debates and views on either Turkey or the EU, rather than on the relationship between them."[7]

The general framework signed by the EU and Turkey in 2005 upon launching accession negotiations is paradigmatic of this distortion. This document states that should Turkey accede to the EU, "long transitional periods, derogations, specific arrangements or permanent safeguard clauses"[8] may have to be considered. The point is rather straightforward: There might be some restrictions on the full participation of Turkey in the EU. Less evident is that behind this linguistic accuracy hide very earthly questions that have been the object of political bickering in Europe for decades.

What is at stake, first, is the money of the European taxpayers. At this stage, any calculation of the financial burden for accepting Turkey into the EU can only be speculative at best, but many in Europe fear that the costs will be prohibitive. Setting a hypothetical scenario for entry into the EU in 2020, for example, a group of European and Turkish economists[9] calculated that as an EU member Turkey could cost as much as .20 percent of the collective EU GDP. That does not appear to be much, but considering that the EU budget ceiling currently stands at around 1.25 percent of the GDP, it would mean that the European citizens who are now receiving hefty subsidies from Brussels will be deprived of a rather considerable piece of the cake. According to the cautious vocabulary above, then, an EU-member Turkey might be cut out of the Structural Funds and the Common Agricultural Policy—the two items currently dominating EU spending.

Second, there is immigration. European citizens of Turkish origins today occupy positions of responsibility, even in national and

European political institutions. The "Euro-Turks"—as they are called—contribute as much as €80 billion ($106 billion) to the European economy.[10] However, deep-seated prejudices dating back to the Turkish *gastarbeiter*, the immigrant workers of the 1960s, are more difficult to do away with. With the Turkish community in Europe already numbering some 3.7 million, the prospect of Turkish membership is a sensitive issue in a number of EU states (especially Germany, which hosts roughly 2.3 million ethnic Turks). The conditions that the EU and Turkey have agreed upon provide for limitations, temporary or permanent, to the movement of Turkish workers within the EU.

The technical conditions can become more political than that. The EU-Turkey framework further states that, "negotiations are an open-ended process, the outcome of which cannot be guaranteed beforehand." This vocabulary insinuates an element of doubt regarding the confidence of the parties in a positive outcome. One can dispute whether it also reflects a genuine concern about the magnitude of the Turkish challenge. What is more certain is that it has vindicated the anti-Turkey lobby in Europe, for whom the battle cry has always been that the EU should aim for a "privileged partnership"[11] with Turkey as an alternative to full membership.

Predictably, the Turkish establishment has flatly rejected any such alternative: "illegitimate and immoral," thundered then Foreign Minister Gül. Technically, he had a point in protesting. Europe is asking Turkey to undergo profound reforms in order to attain membership, and any talk of "open-endedness" undermines that request. Nevertheless, enlargement—especially in the Turkish case—has never been purely technical; it is political, and politics can sometimes be illegitimate and immoral.

FROM HYPE TO APATHY (AND BACK)

This inherent partisanship helps clarify some of the most mind-boggling contradictions in the European take on Turkey. For example, there is the fact that so much of the discourse is focused on Turkey's identity, religion, and geographical position. When Austrians refer to the 1683 Ottoman siege of Vienna to explain their opposition to Turkey, or when politicians, such as former French President Valery Giscard D'Estaing, argue that Turkey's entry into Europe will spell "the end of the EU," it is ideology talking.

Similarly, the transformation of the Turkish democracy may well constitute a model for reform in the Muslim world, as Turkey advocates argue. Accession to the EU may be an invaluable asset to Europe's multiculturalism. Turkey's geographical location can represent a crucial asset for the fortunes of the EU as an international actor. At this stage, however, it is all too easy to dismiss any such argument as guesswork or wishful thinking. The truth is that even if it wanted to, Ankara can do nothing about its history or the religious orientation of its people. Making a case for or against Turkey based on these factors is one sure way for not having a debate at all.

Under more ordinary circumstances, the only irritant here would be that the self-appointed wardens of true European values have assumed the same rigid attitude of the nationalist custodians of the true Turkish identity. But politicization has become the rule rather than the exception, and the increasingly heated reactions within Turkey itself have been a product of this norm.

Consider the row surrounding the Armenian "genocide" issue. The polemic arises from the Armenian claim that in 1915–1916 the Ottoman authorities systematically eliminated as many as 1.5 million Armenians. Not only has Turkey's staunch rejection of the "genocide" claim long poisoned the relations between Turkey and Armenia. The contention has also entered the political arena of the countries hosting the Armenian diaspora. In October 2006, for example, the French National Assembly passed a bill making the denial of the Armenian "genocide" an offence. In so doing, a matter that most sensible people recommend to the work of historians has been turned by some into yet another indication of the anti-Turkey bias in Europe. As a Turkish commentator wrote on that occasion: "The opposition against Turkey in the EU has begun to present an ugly face."[12]

When the EU gave the green light to open negotiations, many Turks were willing to give Europe the benefit of doubt. Ever since then, the prevailing impression has returned to that of Turkey simply not being wanted in Europe. France, in particular, has introduced a clause in its constitution calling for popular referendums for any EU expansion following the accession of Croatia. Even in usually pro-enlargement countries, such as Italy and Britain, support for EU membership for Turkey is at an all-time low.[13] Unsurprisingly, the rates of EU approval in Turkey itself have plummeted from over 70 percent in 2002 to less than 40 percent in 2008.

As much as it indicates the growing opposition to the EU, this decline in Turkish support can also be interpreted as an expression of a more listless disillusionment pervading the Turkish population. The unintended byproduct of excessive politicization may well be that Turks have resigned themselves to their journey toward Europe having no destination.

Perhaps most suggestive of this change of heart is the way in which the accession process itself, and the discussions surrounding it, have sobered. The negotiations—supposedly the embodiment of Europe's objectivity on Turkey—have been a highly disputed matter from the very outset due to the conflict in Cyprus. Ankara, whose troops have occupied the northern, Turkish-speaking part of the island since 1974, refuses to recognize the southern, Greek-speaking part. In order to sanction the lack of progress on this issue, the EU has frozen talks on 8 of the 35 "chapters" of legislation that form the basis of the enlargement talks. Whether because of the anti-Turkish sentiments in Europe or because Greek Cyprus has gained unprecedented leverage on the peace process since entering the EU in 2004, many in Turkey could not help branding the European position as political.

Since that time, the accession negotiations have proceeded at a snail's pace. Thus far, the EU and Turkey have opened talks on 11 "chapters"; by comparison, Croatia started the process at the same time as Turkey and has opened 22 of them. Rather than provoking outrage or inciting anti-European sentiments, however, this stalemate is producing apathy. In the domestic drama that has been unfolding in Turkey over the past couple of years, Europe has played an increasingly marginal role. During the 2007 campaign, national security and constitutional reform were much hotter items of debate than the EU. Since those elections, the reform agenda pursued by the government has lost much of its Euro-enthusiasm. On the occasion of the Constitutional Court case against the AKP, European concerns were barely featured in the media. Even for highly sensitive accomplishments encouraged by the EU, such as the amendment of article 301 of the Penal Code, a widespread attitude appears to be: "I don't care about Brussels. I care about Turkey. And that's why 301 has to go!"[14]

In theory, one should welcome a more sober tone. It is a way to allay the fears that the Turkish EU bid has spawned on both the European and Turkish sides. In other instances of the European project, a lack of popular involvement has turned out to be conducive to bringing complex integration deals forward. Moreover, the enlargement process would certainly benefit from a renewed focus on the substance of the negotiations.

All this would help, but it will not suffice. Once told that the Turkish entry into the EU places the existence of both at risk, the Turkish and European populations will not easily allow themselves to be left behind. Clashes have diminished, but that is because Europe and its offer are losing credibility—not because of any deliberate effort by the political leaders on either of the two sides.

Should enlargement return to the Turkish policy agenda in earnest, so would the hype. More likely still, the economic downturn or a spike of violence with the Kurdistan Workers Party rebels in the country's southeast[15] may again sharpen the nationalist line in government circles.

Like-minded Europeans and Turks can do little to prevent all this from happening, but they can prepare for it.

IF YOU CAN'T BEAT THE PARADOX

In downtown Rome, you are still unlikely to spot a young woman wearing a headscarf. At least for the foreseeable future, you will not hear echoes of the muezzin calling to prayer from a megaphone, nor will you catch sight of a minaret. But take a stroll down İstiklal Avenue, the pedestrian thoroughfare in central Istanbul, and you may be forgiven for feeling you are in the middle of the *Corso* in Rome. From the sticky humidity to the busy shoppers, from its elegant architecture to the St. Anthony Catholic church, İstiklal bears such a striking resemblance to the avenue in the Italian capital that one is reminded why, centuries ago, Istanbul used to be the "Second Rome." Surely, in Erzurum or Diyarbakir in Eastern Turkey, it is reasonable to feel as though you are in another country. But that is hardly different from going to parts of the countryside in Southern Italy.

This seemingly improbable parallel is meant to illustrate one simple point. If the paradoxes surrounding Turkey's European future cannot be overcome, they can be joined. The hope that time will simply dispel these contradictions goes against the experience of the lengthy history of European–Turkish relations. Embracing the paradox may well turn out to be more rewarding than avoiding it.

Even to the casual observer of international relations, it is clear that the Turkish EU bid is a special case in the history of European integration. And so is the impact that its entry will have on the European cultural identity, its foreign policy reach, and its institutional setting. But, in their own ways, each of the past and future expansions of the EU presents unique challenges. The landmark enlargement towards the former-communist countries of Central Europe represented a special case. The expansion towards the war-torn and, in some cases, predominantly Muslim, countries of the Balkans will be a special case. The participation of the United Kingdom in the European integration project was such a special case that it was initially vetoed (by France, incidentally). The EU enlargement to Turkey is a special case as well.

What makes the Turkish case unique is that a country that is historically and culturally *central* is, at the same time, consciously *peripheral*. A figurative pirouette around the Anatolian peninsula quickly reveals the first part of this claim. Turkey is one of the great powers in the Caucasus and in the Black Sea area. Thanks to its strong ethnic and economic ties, it is a crucial gateway to Central Asia, the new Eldorado of Western energy planners.[16] Ankara traditionally wields clout in the Middle East, including Israel. Political scientists Barry Buzan and Ole Wæver have gone as far as categorizing Turkey as one of the three centers of the European power architecture, the others being the EU and Russia.[17]

This centrality provides indeed a suitable angle for analyzing Russia's European policy, which continues to be characterized by a geopolitical and even civilizational posturing that is distinct from—and even opposed to—Europe. The case of Turkey is odd, however, because this country's central heritage has been counterbalanced by its unyielding determination to pursue Westernization. In addition to the EU track, Turkey has been a member of the Organization for Security and Cooperation in Europe since 1973 and of the Council of Europe since its foundation in 1949. In recent years, relations with the United States may have soured over a number of highly sensitive issues, ranging from the Iraq war to Washington's support of the Armenian cause. Yet thanks to its firm place in NATO, Ankara has enjoyed trust and even leverage in Washington, to say nothing of the United States' wholehearted support of Turkey's EU application.

Turkish leaders must have been aware all along that none of this is likely to lead Turkey to a position at the political and cultural heart of Europe. Ankara will never be able (or allowed) to exchange its geostrategic centrality for a place at the core of the European continent. But that has never been the point. Rather, Ankara has aimed at reaffirming in every forum and on every occasion that the only route to Turkey's modernization heads westward.

The battle for modernity currently being waged in Turkey is at the heart of this identity paradox. A go-getting Turkish approach embracing the paradox would make the most of the country's geopolitical potential, not as a way to get back at European humiliations,[18] but rather as a means of nurturing the appeal of its foreign policy centrality. Meanwhile, Ankara would renew its reformist impetus, even by setting out its own schedule for meeting EU conditions—regardless of what the EU will deliberate.

As to Europe, the starting point ought to be that the sensitivities surrounding enlargement will continue to inspire the creativity of the Turkey-bashers. In this respect, it is all the more important to reaffirm what the terms agreed upon by the parties explicitly declare. The EU and Turkey entered a process aimed at making Turkey a member of the European family, not only a friend, and the guide to evaluate that process is Ankara's own attainments.

A franker European approach will also have to acknowledge that the matter has long moved past technicalities. Although Turkey will not access the EU for at least a decade, the European debate is dominated by discussions regarding the social and economic fabric of Europe, its cultural identity, and the future of its cherished diversity. These questions are academic for the time being, and will continue to be so long after Turkey will have entered the EU. But much of the European narrative is mired in apocalyptic projections about an EU-member Turkey.

A European approach that embraces the Turkish contradictions would ponder the opposite—and much tougher—issue: the consequences of a permanent rejection of the Turkish EU bid. By weighing exclusion, one can expose the latent and open Turko-phobia pervading part of the European mindset and put the true ambitions of Europe to the test. Pondering a refusal would also be a way to resume Europe's foundational correlation of its quest for security and ever-deeper integration. A rejection of Turkey could impinge on the stability of the wider European periphery, it could affect European energy supplies, and it would most likely fail to alleviate the European fixation with immigration.

Each of these items is pivotal to the future of Europe, regardless of whether Turkey enters the EU or not. But then again, so much of the debate on Turkey constitutes European soul-searching in disguise. Joining the paradox means taking Europe straight to where its Turkey enigma has always belonged: to the rationale and purpose of the European project.

4

The Remains of the Wall

The stage is the finely decorated Assembly Room of the Cardiff City Hall. The supporting cast is an audience of representatives from five European countries. The leading role is assumed by Michel Platini, former soccer virtuoso and current President of UEFA, the Union of European Football Associations. After months of thorough inspections, interviews, fierce lobbying, and creative public relations campaigns, Platini approaches the podium to deliver the final result. Glancing over his tense audience, he opens the envelope, pauses for dramatic effect, and theatrically reveals the printed sheet with the name of the winner. What follows is a coordinated act of despair and joy. The officials sitting on the right side of the hall shake their heads and shrug their shoulders; the left side explodes in a merry-go-round of incredulous ecstasy.

This was the scene upon the announcement that Poland and Ukraine will jointly host Euro 2012, the European soccer championship. Though widely considered an outsider, the bid was deemed more attractive than those of well-equipped competitors, including Croatia, Hungary, and Italy. It must have also proved more compelling. As the Ukrainian Football Federation President proclaimed, "this is a decisive day for our country. It will provide new opportunities ... as it strives to integrate with Europe."[1]

Countless stories suggest how the game of soccer lifts spirits, transcends barriers, and, according to some, even explains the world.[2] The Cardiff episode certainly adds to this list. The selection procedure became an occasion for high-level diplomacy, policy commitments, and symbolic gestures. Since then, serious concerns have been raised about the ability of these two countries to complete the stadiums and infrastructure necessary in time for the tournament, and Ukraine may have to decline the honor of co-hosting the tournament. Yet, the committee that selected the Polish-Ukrainian proposal chose to gamble on the enthusiasm that Europe still manages to convey and to reward the optimism and hope expressed by these two countries.

Like the UEFA committee, Europe is concerned about the former Soviet republics on its border. It is worried about the structural dysfunctions of their institutions; apprehensive about the flow of drugs, weapons, and people that are trafficked through or from them; and disturbed by the influence Russia exerts over them. Unlike that committee, however, Europe's Eastern policy appears stuck in a state of denial, consisting of conditions that do not match incentives and of deeds that underwhelm words. The EU policy appears to float over a strategic silence that is louder than any explicit rejection. For the time being, Europe is not letting itself be dragged into the business of optimism and hope.

ENDLESS TRANSITION

As the saying goes, Adam and Eve were also thought to be undergoing a transition when they left the Garden of Eden. The 77 million souls populating the westernmost former Soviet republics—Ukraine, Belarus, Moldova, Georgia, Armenia, and Azerbaijan—must sometimes feel the same. Practitioners and academics have dissected their progress toward a market-based system of liberal democracy; they have monitored patterns in the individual cases and applied lessons in a broader, comparative perspective. They have been at it for decades, and the results have been enlightening.[3]

Nevertheless, the maddening question for the peoples in this region must ultimately be, "Transition to what, exactly?" These countries emerged from the ruins of the Soviet empire. Some of them have made remarkable—even heroic—strides toward the standard of democracy to which they all claim to aspire. All of them, however, are still attempting to make sense of the broken pieces of their transition.

The most alluring—and deceitful—chunk is represented by their quest for democratic change. The governments in this region claim to hold free and fair elections. In some cases, like Belarus, this is plainly false. In others, it is more credible and by no means a minor achievement for peoples that have been under the Soviet yoke for the better part of the past century. More spectacularly, when corrupt regimes fall under the peaceful weight of thousands of colored scarves and ribbons, it must be difficult to conceal their much-deserved pride.

These feats have not closed the deep pockets of social and economic decay that plague the region. If anything, the so-called "Colored Revolutions," which in 2003 and 2005 toppled incumbent regimes in Georgia and Ukraine, have made the ugly face of Eastern Europe more visible. One notorious case is that of Moldova; once one of the wealthiest parts of the Soviet Union, Moldova is today renowned for being the most impoverished country in Europe. The annual per capita income stands at $1,187, and some 40 percent of the population lives below the poverty line. The other countries, with figures ranging from $2,186 in Georgia to $3,633 in oil-rich Azerbaijan, are not faring much better.[4]

With endemic poverty comes an almost physiological inclination to a broad range of societal dysfunctions, including mass migration and trafficking of various sorts. For obvious reasons, the data consists mostly of estimates. Up to one-quarter of the Moldovan population is thought to be working abroad. According to the government in Kiev, the Ukrainian exodus amounted to some 2.5 million emigrants between 1991 and 2004. Belarus figures on some top-ten lists of the world's largest weapons exporters, and its regime is embroiled in murky arms trade with rogue regimes worldwide, possibly totaling some $1 billion annually. Hundreds of tons of heroin from Afghanistan are moved through Central Asia and then the Caucasus on the way to Europe.[5]

Unsurprisingly, elections as such have offered no relief to these afflictions, but they have not offered any help in the democratic transition of the region either. Even where the ballot box is not blatantly stuffed, post-Soviet politics hovers perennially in a thick fog of manipulation. Eastern Europe remains the world that analyst Andrew Wilson has dubbed "virtual politics," a reality of " 'clones' and 'doubles' … of parties that stand in elections but have no staff or membership or office, of bankers that stand as Communists, of well-paid insiders that stand as the regime's most vociferous opponents, and of scarecrow nationalists and fake coups."[6]

Moreover, it is a reality in which the basic pillars of good governance are missing. From the ability of the government to implement policies to the quality of the public services to the level of corruption, the standards in Eastern Europe remain appalling. According to the World Bank, the performance of the six former Soviet republics on these issues is not only worse than what is found in the former communist states of Central Europe, it is also worse than in Turkey, the other EU accession countries in the Balkans, and a number of North African states.[7]

Controversial constitutional changes, chaotic privatization plans, and poor tax collection—instances of bad governance in Eastern

Europe abound. The conflicts festering in the region are usually not included in this particular list, but they should be. The decade-long stalemates in Nagorno-Karabakh (involving Armenia and Azerbaijan), Abkhazia and South Ossetia (the entities that broke away from Georgia), and Transnistria (Moldova) have long been referred to as the "frozen conflicts." In reality, these are dormant viruses that have drained the economies and societies of the countries concerned. The situations in Nagorno-Karabakh and Abkhazia originate in serious ethnic grievances. The other cases are either more questionable (South Ossetia) or outright fictitious (Transnistria) in their rationale and justification. But all of them add up to veritable black holes of crime, and have constituted a massive roadblock in relation to the transition of these countries.

The brief war fought between Georgia and Russia in August 2008 over South Ossetia blatantly illustrates this point. The story goes that the Georgian artillery attacked the renegade province, triggering immediate Russian response. Having driven the Georgian forces out of South Ossetia, the Russians subsequently entered the other self-declared statelet, Abkhazia, and then Georgia proper. After five days of hostilities, the Russians and Georgians signed a ceasefire brokered by France, and Russia recognized the independence of the two breakaway entities a few days later.

As we will see in the next chapter, this small war has probably more to say about Russia—and even Europe—than about Georgia. When it comes to Georgia, however, the conflict did simmer in an environment in which the state had long lacked legitimacy and control. The war became inevitable under the leadership of President Mikhail Saakashvili, who was bold enough to reassert some of that control, just as he proved erratic in the buildup and aftermath of the hostilities. The war confirmed the risks of running immature democracies and illustrated a maxim familiar to peace researchers: That countries hanging in the gray zone between democracy and autocracy tend to be more war prone than is the case with mature democracies or stable autocracies.[8]

This combination of pervasive corruption and instability paints a dark and particularly convoluted picture. Common sense could suggest that as long as these problems do not stop draining local societies and their economies, solid and sustainable democratic progress will not be forthcoming in Eastern Europe. Rather than the disease, however, these are the symptoms of the predicament these countries find themselves in. The source of the former Soviet quandary is deeply rooted in the deficiency of the rule of law and its institutions: an independent judiciary, a clear division of powers, a system of checks and balances, and so forth.

As persuasively argued by Fareed Zakaria, these institutions the fundamental pillars of any healthy liberal democracy.[9] They define the frame within which the democratic state is supposed to function and constitute the underlying principle guiding any successful transition. In this equation, others[10] have also factored in the economic development in a given country—a point that is well taken when explaining the present situation in Eastern Europe. The bottom line is that as long as the rule of law does not take root, these former Soviet countries may well hold elections and even stage civic revolutions, but democracy will fail to stick.

THE GATEKEEPERS

As it happens, the rule of law is supposed to be the paramount objective of the European policy in the region. If the EU has fallen short of pursuing that goal, it is primarily because Brussels has deprived itself of the tools that could make a dent in the dysfunctional governance structures of these countries.

In the new EU member states of Central Europe, the European approach did the trick because it locked these countries in the meticulous EU enlargement machine. None of the candidates objected to Brussels' rigor in monitoring their progress and setbacks. None of them questioned the commitment of the EU to ferrying them into Europe. In the former Soviet space, the EU has, in principle, followed a similar logic. Back in the mid-1990s, it sealed partnership and cooperation agreements with each of these former Soviet republics. These agreements were comprehensive in scope. The political and economic desiderata were not fundamentally dissimilar to those negotiated with the Central European states. Since 2003, the EU has given its policy a symbolic aura of Euro-engagement. Brussels cheers the "European aspirations" of these countries, welcomes their "European choice," and supports their "integration into European economic and social structures."[11]

Alas, substance has not followed form. For starters, the EU financial assistance to Eastern Europe has been no match to that delivered to Central Europe. The sum that the EU disbursed to the average Central European citizen before the enlargement was six times greater than the amount transferred to the Eastern European citizen. Between 1991 and 2004, the 10 post-communist countries which would then become EU members received aid in the region of €21 billion ($30 billion). The EU assistance to the westernmost former Soviet states in the same period amounted to some €2.6 billion ($3.5 billion).[12]

More significantly, the EU watered down the rigorous set of penalties and incentives constituting its only tested mechanism to guide their transition to a mature market-based democracy. Barring a blatant violator such as Belarus—against which the EU has imposed sanctions—Europe has never suspended agreements or cut off the flow of funding when these states strayed from their commitments.[13] On the other hand, the EU has only made vague advances about what these countries can aspire to if they complied to the EU rulebook, and it has always stopped short of offering the one thing that some of them yearn for: a prospect of membership in the EU.

The low governance standards and the continuing political instability in Eastern Europe have given the Europeans numerous good reasons for maintaining their present position. However, the two main reasons explaining the lukewarm EU policy have remarkably little to do with the countries themselves. The first traces back to Europe's apprehension about overstretching. The enlargement of the EU to Central Europe, we have seen, has brought with it more or less justified concerns about the Union's decision-making processes, its ability to act, and its legitimacy. More than that, it has led to high expectations on the part of some of the former Soviet states, which have been the first to be slashed by the enlargement fatigue litany.

The more detestable side of this posture is probably behind us. In 2009, one no longer hears an EU Commission President seeing "no reason" for having Ukraine or Moldova in the EU. Nor does one read claims by senior European officials that EU expansion to Ukraine would be tantamount to the United States taking in Mexico.[14] Yet, the best expression that Europe has been able to put on its anxiety is the circumstantial formulas of the EU's Neighborhood Policy.

The second, and not unrelated, reason is of course Russia. The Russian ties to its western neighbors are historical and cultural, as much as they are economic and political. Kievan Rus, the medieval state that grew around Kiev, is considered the cradle of the Russian polity. In Ukraine, almost half of the population speaks Russian at home. Crimea, the country's troubled southern peninsula, is home to a majority of ethnic Russians and to Moscow's Black Sea Fleet.

Even the most fervent Europhile in Eastern Europe will agree that European engagement in the former Soviet space is not really about replacing Russia. Having welcomed into the club Latvia and Estonia—where some 30 percent of the population is made up of ethnic

Russians—a Russian presence in the EU is not necessarily what troubles Europeans either.

Rather, Europe fears the geopolitical aftershock already brought about by the westward drift of some of these countries. During and since the 2008 war with Georgia, for example, Russia has claimed to be protecting its "citizens" in the region, based on a policy of creeping annexation which Moscow had pursued by handing out tens of thousands of Russian passports and pensions in the separatist regions. Before the war, Russia had applied trade sanctions against Moldova and Georgia and had expanded its control over strategic businesses in the former Soviet space.

Then there is energy. Disruptions of oil and gas deliveries from Russia first hit news on the occasion of the January 2006 dispute with Ukraine, when gas supplies to Europe plunged by one-third in one day, and then again with a near-identical crisis in January 2009—always in the middle of winter. But whether because of technical problems (Moscow's principal explanation) or in order to bludgeon its neighbors (a prevalent interpretation in the West) Russia has actually halted the energy flow towards the rest of Europe some 40 times since 1991.[15]

In the 1990s, Western European countries followed a rather unchallenged "Russia first" approach, which ranked relations with Moscow above those with the other former Soviet republics. The strategic relevance of a European–Russian partnership, compared to the negligible weight of the former Soviet republics, used to suffice as an explanation for this approach. Since then, however, the symbolic steps that some Eastern Europeans have taken westward, the increasingly assertive Russian posture as well as the enlargement of the EU to former satellites of Central Europe have all complicated that equation.

In an attempt at simplifying things, some analysts are fond of comparing Eastern Europe to Janus, the double-faced Roman god.[16] The proximity of these countries to Russia against their European aspirations, their ties to Central Europe as well as to the Orthodox East, their torn history and culture—everything about these former Soviet republics seems to point in opposing directions.

When examined through the prism of European threat perception, however, the analogy suggests something more. In ancient Rome, Janus symbolized the correlation between openings and closings, beginnings and endings. But he was also the gatekeeper of war, his daunting mission: to guard peace in the empire and lock out instability.[17] The EU may speak highly of the importance of democratic transition in Eastern Europe and has pledged to strengthen its institutions.

Yet, Europe has been far more preoccupied with the need to secure its own zone of peace, to steer clear of the hazards emanating from the former Soviet space, and to contain a resurgent Russia. The official refrain of the ever-closer integration of Eastern Europe is juxtaposed with an underlying narrative centered on the risks emanating from it. The pull of integration is once again pitted against the centrifugal forces of security. Eastern Europe, just like Janus, has served as the guardian for Europe and its fears.

THE ART OF THE POSSIBLE

No European policy-maker really expects to tackle challenges, such as trafficking and energy security, simply by shutting the door—not on a border that, prior to the 2004 enlargement, registered some 10–15 million border-crossings annually; not in a region through which pass some 25 percent of all the natural gas that Europe consumes.[18] Yet, any measure remotely hinting at the full integration of the former Soviet states remains unpalatable to most Europeans. The European solution to this dilemma is that, as Brussels' diplomats explain it, the current EU policy has become a bit like the music of composer Gustav Mahler: much better than it sounds.

The economic aspect provides an insightful example. Europe has become the main commercial partner of all of these former Soviet republics except Belarus. One way of inducing reform would then be to demand progress in their economic governance standards in exchange for freer trade. Brussels has chosen to go a step further: Its stated objective is now that of gradually integrating the economies of Eastern Europe into the EU on the basis of the Brussels' encyclopedic rulebook. "Deep free trade"—the EU jargon for this Herculean task—will have to be calibrated to the capacity of the countries to adopt and implement these measures as well as to the needs they actually have to adopt them. But it is as such a landmark proposal that scores at least two crucial goals in one move. It sets concrete benchmarks to accompany economic reforms in Eastern Europe, and it anchors the region to the prosperous European market.

The EU is pursuing a similar tack on energy. Between pipeline geopolitics and obscure middlemen, energy has never been an easy target for reform in Eastern Europe. More could be done to support some of these countries as they strive to link up to the massive resources of the Caspian without Russian blessing. At the same time, Brussels is encouraging key Eastern European countries to upgrade their pipeline network and to integrate their energy markets, particularly gas and electricity, with the European market. It has created a European Energy Community for doing so, which is due to be extended to Ukraine, Moldova, and, possibly, Georgia.

The broader question regarding the contribution of Eastern European republics in the EU foreign policy is thornier. For one thing, the EU has come to rediscover in this area what it has historically proven best at carrying out: regional cooperation. In the wider Black Sea area, Brussels can tap into the societal and cultural bonds that have tied the countries in the region together for centuries. And it has rightly realized that transnational challenges—from immigration to pollution—ought to be tackled by all the actions involved, not just bilaterally.

Furthermore, Brussels aspires to have the foreign policies of these countries aligned to the EU positions as much as possible. This alignment is a highly symbolic gesture, as it reinforces the pledge that some of the governments in the region have made to European values and its international commitments. Nonetheless, given the constraints, disagreements, and intricacies that have for years made the EU's Common Foreign and Security Policy punch below its weight, such association does not amount to much in real terms.

In this respect, what the Georgian–Russian war has made clear is that Europe has yet to muster the foreign policy means to seriously tackle the complex conflict stalemates in the region. The EU has striven to strengthen its crisis management mechanisms. It has deployed a mission to assist border control in Transnistria and another one to improve the rule of law in Georgia. Brussels sent a few hundred monitors to the region in the aftermath of the Georgia conflict, and in early 2009 it even deployed monitors at the gas pipeline intersections in Ukraine. However, Europe is far from being the diplomatic and military heavyweight in the region. In fact, with the partial exception of Moldova, Brussels has never even been part of the international formats related to the resolution of the "frozen conflicts."

The European ambition—and, probably, its only hope—has been to shift the paradigm governing these conflicts. The EU has aimed to change the context in which these conflicts have emerged. It has aimed at making Moldova and Georgia more attractive to the inhabitants of Abkhazia, South Ossetia, and Transnistria; Europe more visible to the secessionist entities; and its instruments more accessible. Europe has sought to work "around" the conflicts.[19]

In light of the bloody summer of 2008, this would appear to be a rather tall order. The way Europe expects to fulfill it leads to the final and most excruciating item on the EU agenda: winning hearts and minds. The EU has established a plethora of twinning activities, cross-border cooperation, and cultural initiatives in and with Eastern Europe. Redolent of what Czar Peter the Great did to Russia in the 18th century, Brussels has even funded things such as "Window to Europe," a TV broadcast into secluded Belarus.[20]

The problem is that as long as European citizens continue to feel under siege and those in the region left behind, these initiatives may well end up being counterproductive. A couple of years ago, for example, European media circulated the story of 20 kids from the Ukrainian countryside that braved the gelid winter and traveled 300 miles at their expense to apply for a visa at a European consulate in Kiev. There they were asked to sing outside the consulate building to prove that they really were a folk choir invited to a European festival.[21] When things like this happen, the phrase "cultural exchange" carries more than a hint of sarcasm.

The episode is crude, but it illustrates two imperatives with which Europe has been grappling in recent years. The first concerns young people, a segment of the population that is often instinctively pro-European but has had the misfortune to only live through the post-Soviet hardships. For years, the EU student exchange program has offered a mere 20 places a year to students from Ukraine and 7 to those of Moldova, countries with populations of 46 and 4 million, respectively.[22] This could simply be branded as poor policy, if only the program also was not intended to build a new generation of Europeans, which makes these figures plainly deplorable. Tellingly, then, the EU's recent assistance in this region should enable the enrollment of an estimated 1,000 students every year by 2009.[23]

The second imperative relates to the revision of the visa regime for Eastern European citizens. The EU has reached visa facilitation deals with the more advanced countries in the region in exchange for "readmission" (by which the partner country will take back illegal migrants entering the EU through its borders, even though the migrants are not nationals of the country in question). The new system is expected to only make a difference for specific categories, such as journalists and businessmen. Given the levels of border control in Eastern Europe and the sensitivities within the EU on this matter, Eastern Europeans cannot realistically aspire for more for the time being. Even so, the EU hopes that this single regime will bring about speedier procedures, lower costs, and produce more effective controls. It is also hoped that it will spare Eastern Europeans more humiliating bureaucratic ordeals.

Deeper trade, foreign policy coordination, and closer people-to-people contacts exemplify the application of the most rewarding

European foreign policy approach. These measures, which starting in 2009 will be included in a comprehensive initiative called "Eastern Partnership," mark a gradual comeback for good governance as the centerpiece of the European strategy. They pave the way for a stricter application of conditions and testify to Europe's faith in gradual integration as the best antidote to instability.

Laudable as they may be, these initiatives do not solve the problem that, like Mahler's music, European policy still sounds worse than it actually is. Ask a Ukrainian, a Moldovan, or a Georgian citizen about Europe and its policies towards them, and the most common answers will still most likely contain the words neglect and ambivalence. The underlying impression is still that Europe is eluding the important questions in order to buy itself some time. In Eastern Europe, there is still only one tune that can make the EU policy sound right.

TOO QUIET ON THE EASTERN FRONT

Eastern Europeans crave a signal. Some Central European governments have stepped up lobbying on their behalf. Nevertheless, the taboo relating to their possible integration into Europe has yet to be lifted. On the bright side, it is becoming increasingly difficult to put these six countries in the same basket. Belarus persists on a staunchly autocratic path, although Russia's newfound belligerence has forced President Aleksandr Lukashenka to consider a number of overtures from Europe. Armenia and Azerbaijan continue to oscillate perilously in the undefined zone between democracy and autocracy. Georgia lingers on instability and now struggles to restore some of its democratic credentials. Despite their serious domestic shortcomings, Ukraine upholds its objective of Euroatlantic integration.

The "Atlantic" part of this goal is becoming increasingly problematic. Possibly the most perceptible residue of the Cold War bipolarity is that even the remote possibility of prospective NATO membership for Ukraine and Georgia constitutes the single move that is sure to trigger a hostile reaction from Moscow. Key NATO members such as Germany and France have dug in their heels and opposed the prospects for membership for these countries. Popular support for the Alliance in the region remains mixed. NATO enjoys peaks of support of over 75 percent in Georgia, while the support in Ukraine is somewhere around 20 percent.

After a summit in May 2008, NATO reassured Ukraine and Georgia that they can eventually join, although it passed the buck to the

Obama administration to press the case for Ukraine and Georgia. The conflict in the Caucasus, together with a less confrontational U.S. posture, have made that case weaker in the coming years. The overall consequence is that the unwritten Western strategy of the 1990s, whereby bold NATO engagement paralleled or even paved the way for the EU—an issue explored in greater detail in Chapter 7—may be approaching its natural demise.

When it comes to the EU, it is likely that Europe will offer some of these nations the possibility to enter the Union at some point. If the fading Colored Revolutions have left any legacy, it is that fewer Europeans care to object to the "European identity" of Ukraine or Moldova. For now, however, Europe has wrapped its broad array of measures into formats that are silent about the membership aspirations of these countries. In the short run, this ambiguity may have provided embattled reformers something to show for their pro-Western rhetoric. But judging by the pace of reforms, Europe's fuzziness is not driving the transformation of the region nearly as far and as fast as one could have hoped.

The global financial crisis has made the EU if possible even more introverted, as it has taken one of its heaviest tolls in Eastern Europe. Ukraine, the region's largest player and in many ways its forerunner, has seen inflation rise by 20 percent in 2008, while industrial production fell by as much as a third. After almost a decade of relatively steady growth, the economy is forecast to contract by 5 percent in 2009. Both Ukraine and Georgia have been bailed out by the International Monetary Fund and even Belarus was provided with an emergency loan package.

The situation appears as dire as, if not more, than in some former Soviet satellites of Central Europe, such as Hungary or Latvia. The difference is that the latter nations' membership in the EU has cushioned their worst fears about an economic collapse, about the return of Russia's menacing shadow, or even about the viability of their economic and political transition. These former Soviet republics, instead, have been fully exposed to the sheer power and fallout of the turmoil.

Injecting political confidence is as important as injecting capital. In Eastern Europe, this is ultimately a matter of being publicly and repeatedly clear about the eventual prospects for EU enlargement, while being just as unequivocal that membership is not in the cards any time soon. For a country such as Ukraine, prospective membership would mean a tortuous journey that could end in no less than 15 years. But it would also mean that there is at last a destination and, one can hope, a basis around which its querulous politicians can build a semblance of consensus.[24] For Europe, providing such prospective membership would neither instantly restore its credibility nor would it suddenly reverse the fortunes of its underperforming policy. It would, however, constitute the most direct way to reawaken from its strategic trance.

Russia's Roller Coaster

In 1856, "Russian Foreign Minister" must have been one of the trickiest job titles in the world. During the first half of that century, Russia had defeated France, dictated conditions at the 1815 Congress of Vienna, and proceeded to dominate the European geopolitical scene at the time. In the years leading up to 1856, however, Russia suffered a crushing defeat in the Crimean War, which suddenly gave way to a seemingly disintegrating empire.

Prince Aleksandr Gorchakov took over the Foreign Ministry immediately after that debacle with one single point on his agenda: restoring Russian greatness. He reckoned that in order to regain its place in the Concert of Europe, Russia would have to focus on economic and social recovery; it would have to practice a pragmatic and unassuming foreign policy. After—only after—the state regained its strength, Russia would be back to unremittingly pursuing its true great power ambitions. It took Russia years to execute this plan and reclaim a position of prominence. Gorchakov, however, had it all figured out five months into office. As he wrote in a dispatch to his ambassadors on August 21, 1856, "Russia doesn't sulk, it concentrates."[1]

Fast-forward to 1992. Besides the political, military, and geostrategic losses, the disintegration of the Soviet Union was, above all, a colossal ideological defeat. The economy did not come to the rescue and, in fact, it was a considerable part of the cause. In the early–mid-1990s, the size of the Russian economy was some 4 percent of that of the United States at the time. In 1992, inflation was at 2,500 percent. By 1996, the black economy accounted for about half of the entire Russian output.[2] Then came the financial meltdown of 1998, which delivered the *coup de grace* to the crippled Russian economy.

Then-President Boris Yeltsin not only oversaw all this, he personified it. Reading the obituaries that poured in after his death in 2007, many foreign observers hardly concealed their nostalgia for the Yeltsin years. History might have taken a very different course had he not stood defiantly on that tank in front of the Russian Parliament building in the summer of 1991. Though unpredictable, his presidency conveyed the hope that Russia can also rightfully aspire to be a democracy.

However, it was Yeltsin who crushed the parliamentary opposition. His entourage was responsible for endorsing the unpopular "spinach treatment" of shock financial and economic reforms. By the time he had left office, some of the former Russian vassals in Central Europe were being admitted to NATO; Moscow was forced to swallow over two months of NATO bombings of their Orthodox brethren in Serbia and was practically losing Chechnya. As much as one can feed the myth of a revolutionary hero, Yeltsin's Presidency faithfully reflected the disaster of the country that he ruled.[3]

No wonder that, by the turn of the millennium, the figure of Prince Gorchakov had witnessed a revival in Russia. For many Russians, the single word that best captioned Yeltsin's tenure was humiliation. They could not afford to sulk, and more than just concentration was required to recover. But as Moscow made its way back to the center of the global arena, what stood out from Gorchakov's famous dispatch was not the feeling of history repeating itself; it was the vaguely vengeful undertone.

A WORLD WITH RUSSIA

With Vladimir Putin's election to the Presidency in 2000, a peculiar Russian blend of autarchy and paternalism returned to the helm. The state is in charge, knows what is best, and needs no advice. Little by little, the new leadership systematically disavowed the optimistic credo that Western analysts refer to as "triple transition": to market economy, to liberal democracy, and to independent state- and nation-building. In a strong Russia, power is "vertical," democracy is "sovereign," and the state is governed by a "dictatorship of the law"—with an accent on the first term, as it turned out.

The President's own background goes a long way to explaining this terminology and how his administration has used it. A former KGB agent and head of its successor agency, Putin has beefed up the Russian power structures with loyalists and former colleagues. The *siloviki* ("men of power"), as they are known, have been appointed to run anything from the state-owned oil company to the national railroads.[4] The KGB does not run Russia, as is sometimes assumed; in the unforgiving milieu of Russian politics, reliance on only one political faction can, quite literally, turn out to be lethal. Even so, blatant opponents of the regime, including many members of Yeltsin's "family," have become an endangered species, some of them confined to the posh neighborhoods of London, others to Siberian prisons.

From the clamp-down on political opposition to the jailing of bothersome businessmen, evidence attesting to Russia's autocratic involution abounds. Perhaps what testifies to it most crudely remains the disturbing aftermath of the Beslan school siege in September 2004. Disturbing not because of the Chechen terrorists that carried out the mission or because of the Russian Special Forces that stormed the school and exterminated the hostage-takers together with dozens of captive children. That was all downright atrocious. The Beslan bloodshed was disturbing because it provided the Kremlin the occasion to announce a number of questionable administrative reforms.

After Beslan, the Russian Federation virtually ceased to be a federation, as regional governors were effectively nominated by the Kremlin. Moreover, the Kremlin abolished single-mandate representation districts in the lower house of Parliament.[5] Lawyers can wrestle, as they did, regarding the constitutionality of these changes. But the truly baffling question concerned the link between these reforms and the Beslan massacre. Chris Patten, the sharp-tongued EU Commissioner for External Relations at the time, responded for many when he feared that "the only answer to terrorism is to increase the power of the Kremlin."[6]

This strengthening of the Russian state has not made Russian society—or its citizens, for that matter—any more robust. According to the Russian statistics service, the murder rate has increased during Putin's first term compared to the previous four years. The life expectancy of Russian men has fallen below 59 years of age. One million people (over 1 percent of the adult population) live with HIV/AIDS—one of the most rapidly developing epidemics worldwide—and alcoholism kills 40,000 Russians annually. As scholars Michael McFaul and Kathrin Stoner-Weiss have argued: "Given the growth in its size and resources, what is striking is how poorly the Russian state still performs…. Russians are actually worse off today than they were a decade ago."[7]

This notwithstanding, exactly one decade ago, a prominent Russia observer could still reasonably argue that, "it is only prudent that we begin to contemplate a world without Russia."[8] Over the past years, the opposite has been true and has been no platitude. We have been contemplating a world *with* Russia. At the beginning of his tenure as President, Putin vowed to double the size of the Russian economy by 2010. Thanks in large part to skyrocketing oil prices throughout much of the present decade, he has more than delivered. Until the 2008 financial crisis at least, Russia had been sailing at average levels of growth of about 7 percent a year. The international debts accumulated following the collapse of the Soviet Union have been repaid. Pensions and salaries have been paid on time, and tax collection has improved. Moscow has become one of the most expensive cities in the world, populated by an expanding breed of outrageously wealthy millionaires. It is hardly surprising that Putin and his handpicked successor, Dmitry Medvedev, have consistently enjoyed approval ratings between 70 and 80 percent.

Above all, in the minds of its rulers, a world with Russia is one in which this immense Euro-Asian landmass stretching from Kaliningrad in Central Europe to the easternmost tip of Asia in Vladivostok is no longer *terra incognita*. It means that Russia is rediscovering Asia, where the country's depopulating eastern region borders up against the rising ambitions of China. Russia is returning south, strengthened by its traditional ties with Central Asia, its influence in the Middle East, and its growing Muslim community.[9] And it is returning west, not (necessarily) on the strength of its nuclear arsenal, but rather on that of its enormous energy reserves and an aspiration to redesign the normative and geopolitical contours of Europe.

ALWAYS A RIDDLE

Europeans could never possibly act as disinterested bystanders of this recurrent rollercoaster ride.[10] Throughout history, they have engaged in heated discussions about its significance and implications. Jean-Jacques Rousseau, for one, thought that "Russia will never be civilized." The German thinker Friedrich Engels believed that Russia "became a European country like any other." After being shown the map of occupied Germany after World War II, Churchill is said to have quipped, "Are we going to let these barbarians right into the heart of Europe?"[11] Whether as the unruly learner that needed or wanted to be part of the European civilization, or the ruthless enemy that threatened the survival of that civilization, Russia has always been something of an alter ego to Europe.

The echoes of these utterances reverberate in today's bilateral relations. The EU and Russia are the largest geopolitical animals on the European continent.[12] Its leaders have long spoken of the bilateral relations in terms of a "strategic partnership." For some statesmen and observers, this is reminiscent of the Gaullist vision of a *Grande Europe*, a space united by common historical ties and a joint geopolitical future. More humbly, a strategic partnership has been motivated by the fact that the two parties are each other's major counterparts on the continent in most fields of cooperation. Unfortunately, the EU and Russia can hardly be seen as partners, and the "strategic" attribute is greatly misleading.

It is difficult to shrug off the feeling that the Europeans have brought this state of affairs upon themselves. The EU policy towards Russia has been a cacophony of multiple voices, ranging from the deferential whisperings of some Western European countries, to the Russo-phobic bawling by the former Warsaw Pact members in Central Europe. This division reflects important differences in the history of European countries and of their often complex relations with Russia, but it is also a product of conflicting interests.

Large, state-controlled energy companies in Italy, France, and Germany are among the best partners of Gazprom.[13] Several European countries (such as Finland, the three Baltic states, the Czech Republic, Slovakia, and Bulgaria) receive between 75 and 100 percent of their gas from Russia. Various EU institutions, including individual departments within the European Commission, run their own tiny Russia policies on individual issues. Relations with Moscow have been a textbook case of Europe's often intangible foreign policy.

To be sure, Russia has hardly been standing still. Notwithstanding its ignorance on EU matters, Russia has been extraordinarily adept at pitting EU institutions against its member states, and member states against one another. By relying on bilateral relations with trusted countries, Russia has bypassed EU institutions—paralyzing the already lukewarm European action. As this tactic succeeds, a widespread sense of contempt for the inefficient and patronizing EU has ended up pervading Russia. According to a 2007 poll, 70 percent of the Russian population does not feel "European," and almost 50 percent of all Russians perceive Europe as an economic threat.[14]

It has not always been this way. In 1994, the EU and Russia signed a partnership and cooperation agreement not very different from those that the EU sealed with the other former Soviet republics. While Russia could never possibly be a mere European neighbor, the chaos presided over by Yeltsin made a mildly "Europeanizing" path appear justified.

More interestingly, foreign policy views within Russia itself were then more fluid than they are today. After all, it was none other than

Andrei Kozyrev, the Russian Foreign Minister of the day, who requested assistance "to set [us] on our feet and become a normal member of the European Community."[15] A Russian Foreign Minister making such a request today might well find himself relocated to some faraway embassy.

In the Russia of today, partnership with Europe can no longer imply imitation, inferiority, or humiliation. Bilateral relations, says Moscow, follow a syllogism that goes something like this. Russia fills European pipes with its natural gas (about 40 percent of the total European imports). European countries collectively are Russia's first trading partners (over half of its total exports, and about 45 percent of its imports). *Ergo*, Russia and the EU are mutually dependent. This justifies the Kremlin's emphasis on a partnership of equals between the EU and Russia and its desire to negotiate specific rules tailored to their unique relationship.

Eyes should roll at the logic of this argument. For one, the EU and Russia are indeed different political animals: a complex institutional organization facing a traditional nation-state. Furthermore, the claim that Russia and Europe are equal is questionable on the grounds of sheer size. Without stable European demand, it would have been unthinkable for Russia to sustain the growth rates of the recent years. And although the Russian economy has been thriving in recent years, it is still smaller than a mid-sized power such as Spain.

Nevertheless, Europe has seemingly bought into the equality argument. European countries that are more lenient towards Russia (or dependent on its gas) defend bestowing privileged status on Moscow as the price to be paid for a reliable and engaged partner. Critics, instead, refer to one of the worst European traditions: appeasement. What seems clear from the viewpoint of the Kremlin is that if the EU and Russia are indeed peers, then reciprocity applies. There is to be no condescending or double standards, and meddling in each other's affairs will no longer be tolerated.

Regardless of whether one considers this to be engagement or appeasement, this is where the EU Russia strategy freezes. The European drumbeat of economic reforms and rule of law only works when a country bows to the superiority of the EU rules and conditions. The moment Russia departs from this framework, Europe is instantly checkmated.

The cherished reference to "common values" offers a case in point. Whenever Europeans have criticized, say, human rights abuses in Chechnya, it has become routine to hear Russian officials citing the levels of corruption and conflicts of interest within Europe. Or referring the word "mafia," which, as Putin once retorted to Italy's Romano Prodi, was not invented in Russia. Such instances may have contributed to Putin's rock-star status at home, but they have also rendered the discourse as grotesque as only some Russian literature can be.

Moscow has repeated this basic tactic *ad nauseam* in recent years. In 2007, Russia suspended the application of the Conventional Forces in Europe Treaty—an arms control agreement—in response to the prospective deployment of the U.S. missile defense system in Poland and the Czech Republic. The same year, the Kremlin shut offices of the British Council in Russia in retaliation for a British investigation of the murder of Aleksandr Litvinenko, a former Russian spy who had been granted political asylum in Britain. And then the Baltic states and their mistreatment of their Russian-speaking minorities, Denmark and its presumed support for the Chechen cause, or even Poland and the quality of its meat exports to Russia—every occasion has provoked a show of force, proving that Russia can take on individual European countries, thereby deriding Europe's institutional mechanisms.

The chilling corollary to this situation is that Russia has turned the tables on the normative basis of post-Cold War Europe. At face value, Russia has indulged the EU in its narrative about open borders, and shared norms. Tellingly, the bilateral relations are implemented on the basis of a document titled, "Common Spaces," which concerns cooperation in fields including economic integration, internal security, external security, and culture. Russia's real posture, however, is about anything but common spaces; it is about rigid fault-lines, exclusive spheres of influence, and a God-given right to a "near abroad."

In this sense, the good work of the political "technologists" in the Kremlin has gone far beyond muscle-flexing in relation to neighbors. Russia has offered visa-free regimes and open labor markets to its more compliant friends. It has supported non-governmental movements and financed Russia-friendly mass media in the former Soviet space. Russia's own neighborhood strategy is about revisionism. It is about declaring out loud the long unspoken belief that the demise of the Soviet Union was not a defeat, but a temporary aberration. It is about recreating the other pole of European attraction centered in Moscow. As Mikhail Gorbachev—whose reformist leadership indirectly contributed to the collapse of the Soviet Union—has recently written, it is about building "a united Europe not only from the west but also from the east."[16]

THE GEORGIAN SEAL

Much has changed since Russian tanks rolled across the Georgian border on August 8, 2008. Things have changed for the government in Tbilisi, which is now facing a daunting reconstruction plan (though graciously sponsored by the international community). Georgia has lost any residual chance to reunite with its breakaway statelets for the time being. Things have changed for some 60,000 refugees who have scattered throughout the war zones.

All the same, little has really changed. The conflict and its aftermath have not marked a dramatic change in relation to Moscow's foreign policy posturing of the recent years. Europe has not overhauled its stance on Russia because of it. The conflict has not even radically impacted the balance of power in the Caucasus. What the war *has* accomplished is to make explicit a geopolitical shift that had been subtly consolidating for at least half a decade.

Russia, no doubt, has paid a price for its choices. Its well-orchestrated propaganda campaign has mostly bombed. The reference to genocide and ethnic cleansing allegedly perpetrated by the Georgians or to Moscow's "responsibility to protect"[17] Russian citizens in the Caucasus may have worked in the domestic context, but it failed to convince almost everyone outside it. Nicaragua is the only country in the world besides Russia to have recognized the independence of the two separatist regions. Even Russia's supposed allies in Central Asia and China have steered clear from endorsing Moscow's actions in the war.

On the other hand, the tandem now ruling Russia—with Putin, who became Prime Minister in May 2008, flanked by President Medvedev—must have drawn the conclusion that the gamble has largely paid off. None of the worst-case scenarios—from economic sanctions to the expulsion of Russia from international forums, such as the G-8, to Western military retaliation—has materialized. In fact, the conflict has enabled Russia to call the Western bluff in Eastern Europe.

The West, the United States in particular, had been quick to support the Georgian government and even to train its military until as late as one month before the war. However, most of what the United States ended up doing in the event of the conflict was to fly the troops that Tbilisi had contributed to Iraq back to Georgia and to off-load some humanitarian relief aid in the immediate aftermath of the war. Western countries only condemned what is customarily defined as the "disproportionate"[18] use of force (read, Russian occupation of several towns in Georgia proper). One is left wondering whether we would have heard anything at all had Moscow's military response been deemed "proportionate."

When it comes to Europe, many observers have rejoiced that, during the war, the rotating EU Presidency happened to fall on a powerful state such as France. Were it not for President Sarkozy's febrile shuttling between Tbilisi and Moscow, the war could have dragged on longer. It was anything but far-fetched to imagine such conflict expanding to the inflammable regions and countries surrounding Georgia. Europe, said German Foreign Minister Frank Walter Steinmeier, acted as the "honest broker," in the event. More than that, added the French President himself, European responsiveness showed how much the EU can attain with better foreign policy coordination (which would be one of the main innovations of the EU Reform Treaty).[19]

Well, how much did Europe attain? The contenders declared to have signed different versions of the ceasefire brokered by France. One of the agreement's six points (hotly contested by the Georgians) even gave the Russian "peacekeepers" the right to put "additional security measures" in place until a yet-to-be-determined international mechanism was in place. Moscow is planning the establishment of military bases in both Abkhazia and south Ossetia. Rather than the honest broker, Europe acted as the notary of the Russian occupation.

The itchier question, however, concerns whether Europe's role is at all meant to be that of an honest broker. Europe has played the role of the neutral actor that takes no side and mediates between warring parties. But that reading overlooks the fact that the EU had also styled itself as the standard-bearer of a peaceful and borderless Europe. What stands out about the Georgian–Russian conflict is that the prospects for Russian citizens to be able to travel more easily to Europe did not put off Russia's defiant posture. The looming financial turbulence did not dissuade Moscow from launching the first direct attack on a foreign nation in 30 years. The prospect of closer integration or freer trade did not even deter little Georgia from its reckless military plans.

As Bulgarian scholar Ivan Krastev has rightly argued, this was "the first 19th-century war in 21st-century Europe."[20] What the war sanctioned was that, at least in this part of the continent, the European model of inclusion and integration is still not able to prevail over balance of power and open confrontation. The EU as such may not have emerged from the war as defeated, but that very kind of Europe that the EU is meant to promote certainly did.

LEARNING JU-JITSU

Fyodor Dostoevsky once said that, "being a true Russian will ultimately mean bringing reconciliation to Europe's contradictions."[21]

Europe's contradictions have apparently been a constant throughout the centuries. And according to its present rulers, the assertive Russia of today is certainly truer than that of the 1990s. What is less plain is that Moscow's assertiveness can indeed provide one notable incentive to a European "reconciliation" of sorts.

Russia's European policy has long been reactive rather than proactive. It has mostly left it to its European counterparts to make proposals and take initiatives regarding the width and depth of the relations. Russia has possibly perfected the practice of retorting to Europe's moves with proportional responses. More recently, Russia has taken the game to a different court. Moscow may lack the "Big Idea" capable of matching the appeal of liberal democracy and drawing allies voluntarily to its side. But the basic logic of realpolitik has proven solid enough for Moscow to advance its own vision of Europe. Russia is becoming proactive rather than merely reactive.

The energy sector, the bedrock of Russia's confidence, has been paradigmatic of this shift. When it was weak and cash-strapped, Russia could not but agree to meet Europeans on their home-turf of laws and rules. Moscow signed agreements such as the 1994 Energy Charter Treaty, regulating the energy relations among over 50 states. During a decade in which oil has for some time hovered above $100 per barrel, Russia has become stronger, has amassed as much as half a trillion dollars in gold and foreign currency reserves, and has made any such agreement obsolete simply by ignoring it.

The proactive side of the story is that the game has shifted to pipelines—a game that Moscow, and Gazprom in particular, seems to master. Russia is systematically preempting any European move aiming at "diversification"—one of the European goals being the reduction of its energy dependence on the same foreign producers. To that end, the EU supports the construction of an ambitious pipeline called "Nabucco" (as in the Verdi opera where an oppressed people is liberated), which would take gas from Central Asia into Central Europe. Russia has backed a rival project, South Stream, and has secured, one by one, the support of Italy, Austria, Bulgaria, and Serbia. A consortium chaired by former German Chancellor Gerhard Schröder is set to build Nord Stream, a pipeline running along the seabed of the Baltic Sea from Russia directly into Germany. Moscow has forwarded the idea of a gas cartel bringing other producers together, including Iran and Qatar, and has even anticipated the EU in exploring, producing, and transporting gas from Nigeria. The European energy agenda is not being set by common rules, but by Russia's alliance-building and divide-and-rule policy—to which many European nations appear happy to oblige.

This go-getting activism is expanding to the European power constellation as a whole. Rather than bickering with NATO from the sidelines, Russia has proposed the creation of a new European Security Treaty. Instead of assuaging the international bodies assigned to resolve the conflicts in the Caucasus, the Kremlin changes the facts on the ground, as the Georgian war made clear. Success in this revisionist venture is all but assured and Moscow's proposals often look highly improbable. But Russia is officially on the offensive.

Unexpected as it may sound, this tactical realignment can actually turn out to be quite congenial to Europe. During the Georgia crisis, all 27 European states found themselves in the pleasantly unfamiliar position of agreeing—with a speed unknown to EU foreign policy procedures—on the immediate suspension of the negotiations of a new partnership agreement with Russia. In response to Moscow's aggressive energy policies, the European Commission introduced a so-called "Gazprom clause" as a part of an energy strategy aimed at better integrating the European energy market and at reducing the influence of external actors.

In a more familiar European fashion, both initiatives were, in due course, watered down by compromises and backroom deals. And in any case, it would be illusory to expect that a proactive Russia is all it takes for Europe to finally close ranks and forge bold, common foreign policy positions. But they offer a glimpse of how Europe can respond in a more unified and targeted manner. In this respect, foreign policy does not differ substantially from other aspects of European integration. Europe's tiresome consensus-building procedures require a trigger in order to generate some sense of unity. The increasingly confrontational nature of the Russian moves has provided one.

The Russian roller coaster may soon be on the move again—downward this time. Increase in unemployment, high inflation, and devaluation of the ruble have together presented a serious challenge to Moscow's leadership in the last year. A protracted economic recession, Gazprom's huge foreign borrowings, and a sustained decline in oil prices might well significantly weaken Russia. Europeans now know that the unspoken ambition of shaping the Russian domestic transformation according to their own standards has ground the EU policy to a halt. But they also know that they cannot afford a repeat of the Cold-War containment that some hawks in Central Europe seem to advocate.

Europe needs to do business with Russia, but needs not sell short the values upon which it was founded. The pride that Russia attaches to its global comeback can be tied to the things that the Europeans cherish the most. And at a time when the Russian leadership might again be inclined to lend an ear to reformist voices, a responsive EU can achieve the kind of qualified engagement that Europe—and the whole international community—needs from Moscow. Europeans need to be reminded that, with a heavy dose of pragmatism, Dostoevsky's prediction may not be that far off the mark.

6

A Sea of Troubles

An old Moroccan legend has it that Alexander, the great king of Macedon, once received a complaint from the people of Andalusia, in southern Spain. They were desperate about the continuing devastation and pillaging at the hands of the North African Berbers and pleaded with him to do something about it. Alexander convened his best engineers and ordered them to dig a huge channel between Spain and Africa. The Strait of Gibraltar thus came to be, the Mediterranean basin filled up, and the Andalusians found security happily ever after.[1]

For decades now, European politicians have unabashedly played the tune of togetherness uniting the Mediterranean region. The sea, they will tell you, is the cradle of the European civilization: the region where, as French historian Fernand Braudel put it, "to live is to exchange." The Mediterranean is the place where Europe has spun the Latin notion of the *mare nostrum* ("our sea") into an inspired rhetoric of civilizational cross-fertilization. As a high-level advisory group set up by the European Commission proclaimed in 2003, there is "certainty that the principal complementarities of the two halves of the Euro-Mediterranean area will, in the next half-century, have been integrated into their day-to-day life."[2]

Sadly, the story of Alexander is a more accurate depiction of the reality facing Europe in the Mediterranean. The European imagery has not found fertile ground on the Southern Mediterranean shores. The tired refrain of North Africa's approximation to Western standards has been trumped by the region's stagnation into underdevelopment and autocracy. The lyrical legacies that Europe claims to have inherited from this region have mixed with the more familiar discourse centered on threats emanating from the backyard.

The Mediterranean is not the springboard of Europe's vision of a wider continental order of stability and prosperity. It is not where the EU has breathed new life into an ancient and rich heritage, but instead an area of deep-seated divides. In this region, Europe's unstated doctrine of increased security for itself in exchange for the integration of its neighbors remains most inconclusively at a loss. For the EU's southern neighbors, the Mediterranean is the hard underbelly of Europe. As far as European public opinion is concerned, it looks as if it should be.

THE TIES THAT DON'T BIND

With an uncanny parallel to that Moroccan legend, the most infamous symbol of Europe's Mediterranean divide is probably Ceuta, the Spanish outpost on the northern coast of Morocco. There, Alexander's channel has taken the shape of a 20-foot-high, razor-wire wall erected by the Spanish authorities. The threat of the Berbers is replaced by the gripping stories of the hundreds attempting to cross the borders on their way into Europe. The wall has not given Europe any peace, and Ceuta and the Canary Islands, Melilla (also in Spain), the island of Lampedusa (Italy), and Samos (Greece) have seemingly turned the Med into Europe's own Rio Grande.

Immigration is an issue that pops up in relation to most of the countries in the European neighborhood. The figures for Mediterranean immigration are not in themselves more staggering than those of the other regions. The scenes of dehydrated, new "boat people" on the beaches of Southern Europe are gruesome—especially when thinking about the brutal treatment many of them receive before and after landing. Still, they account for a minimal fraction of the migrants entering the EU, legally or illegally, every year.[3]

Yet, the Mediterranean has become the archetypal breakpoint of Europe's position on immigration, because it represents the reverse of the dysfunctional multiculturalism within Europe itself. When it comes to Europe's southern periphery, indeed, the issue is sensitive—when not explosive—with respect to Europe's Muslim minorities. Muslims in Europe make up an extremely heterogeneous group, now numbering some 15 million.* In the Netherlands and France, Muslims make up an estimated 5.5 and 9 percent of the population, respectively. Over 6,000 mosques dot the map of Europe,

---

*An obvious but fundamental disclaimer here is that not all Muslims are Arabs, and not all Arabs come from Southern Mediterranean countries. In Europe's increasingly heated security discourse, the first category often ends up conflated with the second one. Especially in some Southern European countries, the first and second categories are conflated with the third one.

and together with repeated episodes of discrimination and urban violence, crises over headscarves and crises over cartoons have fed the
myth of the alleged expansion of "Eurabia."

The inflow of migrants and the cracks in Europe's social architecture represent more than two important public policy issues. In
Europe's collective perception, they embody the most visible facets
of a strategic impasse that ends up coalescing around Europe's
southern backyard. Two intertwined arguments dominate this
twisted Mediterranean narrative: one is socioeconomic, the other
sociopolitical.

On the socioeconomic side, unemployment, poor education, and
housing conditions top the list of the main concerns among European Muslims, and with good reason. In the French *banlieues*, the
desolate Muslim-populated suburbs that were the theater of violent
riots in 2005, unemployment is at almost 20 percent, double the
national average, and reaches 30 percent for youths in their 20s. In
Denmark, which attracted the global spotlight in 2006 subsequent to
the publication of a number of cartoons lampooning the Prophet
Mohammed, the level of educational achievement is "low" for 59
percent of immigrants with Muslim backgrounds. Numbers add to
the picture, with the Muslim population living in Europe projected
to double over the next 20 years, without counting Turkey, Albania,
or Bosnia as possible EU members.[4]

In North Africa and the Middle East, the population is also
expected to grow from the present 280 million to nearly equal that
of Europe with some 400–450 million inhabitants by 2020. Remittances from citizens working abroad comprise the largest amount as
a percentage of the GDP among developing regions. Unemployment
reaches double-digit rates in most cases and less than one-third of
women contribute to the labor force.[5] In other words, while the gulf
between Europe and its Southern Mediterranean partners is widening the Muslims of Europe share a number of concerning trends
with their Southern Mediterranean counterparts.

This argument preludes to the more controversial sociopolitical
dimension. Here also, the roots of the fix on the two shores of the
Med appear different. As the oft-quoted *Arab Human Development
Report* has documented, the Southern Mediterranean countries suffer
from a long-standing "freedom deficit." Authoritarian regimes are
resilient and increasingly sophisticated throughout the region. Dis-
sent is crushed, the judiciary is corrupt, political rights and civil liberties are severely limited.

Within Europe, the cause of the discontent lies principally in the
lack of the identification of Muslim communities with their respective

states. A 2006 Pew Research poll found that—with the partial exception of France—those who identify themselves as "Muslims" greatly outweigh those who feel like citizens of the countries they live in: by 81 to 7 percent in Britain; 69 to 3 percent in Spain; and 66 to 13 percent in Germany.[6]

At the same time, Muslims have cultivated deep and durable ties across the Med. From a European perspective, these particularly concern the role of Islam and its many political variants. Islamism is a rising social force throughout the European South and Southeast Mediterranean rim, spanning from pro-government positions of the Justice and Development Party in Morocco to the extremisms of Hamas, the Palestinian group, and Hezbollah, the powerful Shia movement in Lebanon.

In Europe, hundreds of moderate Islamist associations have mushroomed since the 1960s. These groups started as chapters of the movements in their respective motherlands and used Europe as a podium from which to denounce repression by regimes in the Middle East and North Africa. Over time, they have morphed into the self-appointed spokespersons for Muslims in Europe, interacting with the authorities of the states hosting them.

This is no minor shift, but rather than severing the link with the South, it may have simply changed the name of the game. As these more institutionalized groups paid for their dealings with European states with a decline in their credibility, the blander Sufi movements— with their long-standing political connections with Morocco and Lebanon—have become increasingly popular. And, to a lesser extent, so have the more missionary and militant Salafists, with their resentment for the plight of the Palestinians and the Iraqis.

The question of Muslim radicalization cannot be overstated. It has exposed the severe shortcomings of the European models of integration of migrants. It has challenged the prevailing European wisdom on counter-terrorism, thinking that had long tended to regard terror in terms of a crime problem. It has thrived on the alienation of young, second-generation immigrants.[7]

Muslim radicalization represents a serious issue, especially on the grounds that it has made an all too tempting fit with the alarming tones pervading the public discourse in Western Europe. Also according to that same 2006 Pew survey, 76 percent of the British respondents and 77 percent of the French ones felt concerned by the rise of Islamic extremism in their countries. A full 80 percent and 73 percent of British and French Muslims are worried about their future in those countries.[8] In Europe, "Islamo-phobia" has got its semi-official definition: "a shorthand way of referring to dread and hatred of Islam—and, therefore, to fear or dislike of all or most Muslims."[9] And it does not help that some of the deadliest terrorist attacks in recent years—from Paris '95 to Casablanca '03 and Madrid '04—bore the fingerprints of estranged North African immigrants living in Europe.

Preachers, activists, and scholars have long advocated—with some success—the emergence of a "European Islam," according to which traditions and conventions ought to be molded in order to facilitate the active participation of European Muslims in the societies they live in. Increasing international attention has also been turning—with less success—to the role that moderate, socially rooted Islamist movements can play as a counterweight to the autocracies in the region.[10] More generally, this gloomy record neither underscores a "culturalist" argument, whereby the Arab-Muslim world is seen as owing its troubles to having largely missed out on the enlightened modernization that the West has undergone. Nor is it about tracing and blaming the Mediterranean predicament on the European colonial past of exploitation and oppression.

This kind of north–south dynamic just provides the illustration of a kind of Mediterranean interdependence that, from a European standpoint, is increasingly conflictual rather than cooperative, as it was otherwise meant to be. The brewing set of real or inflated Mediterranean threats has trumped the European aspirations of an emerging area of fruitful interplay. Rather than being divided, the result is that the Med is umbilically joined together in ways that Europe was not longing for.

The EU may have long sought to turn this unconstructive relationship around. For over a decade now, however, its policy has fed into it. European policy-makers argue that their way was always paved with good intentions. Officials in North Africa rebut that the European policy was bound to fail all along. They both have a point, and an unlikely flashback at the opposite end of Europe illuminates the reason why.

THE DAUNTING DÉTENTE

The Kalastajatorppa Hotel in Helsinki overlooks the placid waters of the Gulf of Finland. Through the backdoor, guests can access a tidy, gently sloping beach, from where they can take a walk into the silent woods surrounding the Finnish capital. In the summer of 1975, this was one of the settings chosen to seal a landmark rapprochement among the United States, Europeans, and Soviets: 35 countries in all.

The deal was reached around three "baskets" of cooperation on political, economic, and so-called "human" relations. This formed the
basis for the Conference for Security and Cooperation in Europe,
which largely endures to this day.[11]

The therapeutic effects of that setting on the existential divisions
between the East and West inspired EU policy-makers to arrange
their Mediterranean policy in the exact same fashion. Since 1995, the
Euro-Mediterranean Partnership, also known as the "Barcelona
Process," convenes all of the countries around the basin, a mastodon
of some 39 partners in all.[12] They are bound together by a format of
cooperation, which is also shaped around three baskets: political
and security-related, economic and financial, cultural and social.
Such evocative form was intended to match the strategic substance
of the initiative. The mid-1990s were years of deep European
engagement with Central Europe. After some 20 years of comparably feeble interaction with the Arab-Muslim world, the southern
EU member states grasped the need to rebalance the European out-
reach. The Helsinki-inspired symbolism was meant to signal that
the fall of the Berlin Wall would not only dissolve Europe's eastern
borders. It was to mark the rise of a Europe that would finally
unleash its foreign policy potential and its vision of a wider, undi-
vided continental zone of peace and prosperity—including the
Mediterranean.

But Barcelona has not turned out to be another Helsinki. The EU
has given a reasonably clear indication of its requests by negotiating
bilateral deals with most of the states along the southern shores. Financial assistance has been much less than what the Union had
poured into Central Europe in the 1990s, but the real gap is not measured in terms of money. It is in the fact that, in Central Europe, Brussels correlated deeper economic ties with the reform of the judiciary,
the protection of minorities, and respect for human rights.

Tighter political engagement has never been particularly attractive for most Southern Mediterranean regimes, and where it was
attractive, it has worked up to a point.* Brussels has ended up
accepting the standard alibi made by Arab autocrats who argue
that reforms on their part would pave the way for takeovers by
Islamic extremists (an alibi, by the way, that probably holds true
in the political environment of some of these countries). The EU

---

*Morocco holds the dubious record of being the only country in the world to see its appli-
cation for EU membership flatly rejected on the grounds that the country is not
"European."

has, thus, favored economic cooperation in the hope that more widespread prosperity would eventually spill over to deeper political reforms.

To be fair, Europe's troubles do not stem from that approach in itself. EU countries are North Africa's largest trading partner, so economic cooperation makes good sense. Financial assistance and macro-economic programs in the Mediterranean have been co-financed by the International Monetary Fund and follow standards set by the World Bank. Hence, the charge that economic support should not precede—but rather accompany—political reforms on the receiving end pertains to the EU no less than to other institutions.[13]

The trouble is that Brussels' overly ambitious plan has rendered Europe's operational shortcomings crudely evident. North African officials are hardly ecstatic about the prospect of trade liberalization with the EU. Far more likely is that one will hear them lamenting European protectionism on, most notably, agricultural products and textiles. They will remark that there are faint prospects for the EU objective of a Mediterranean Free Trade Area by 2010. They will corroborate their perception of Europe's arbitrariness with the bilateral oil and gas deals that continue to flow between EU member states and Libya or Algeria.

The inconsistencies on the economic front pale before the paralysis in the security sphere. Here, stalled reforms in the Arab-Muslim world are only worse than the repeated failures of major European confidence-building initiatives. It was not only bad timing that, after the second Palestinian *intifada* (uprising) in 2000, the EU and its Mediterranean partners had to put off their ambitious "Charter for Peace and Stability." An ideological clash alone cannot be responsible for thwarting their attempts to agree in 2005 (sadly, the "Year of the Mediterranean") on a common definition of terrorism. These instances unto themselves are grave blows. But they are also part of a pattern in which an overall strategic misjudgment has been coupled with underperforming execution.

Nowhere has this combination been more detrimental than in relation to the Arab–Israeli conflict. The EU has formally separated its Mediterranean policy from the Middle East peace process. That may seem odd, as the overall goal is to foster a pan- regional zone of peace and stability. But there is logic to it. For one thing, the EU Med policy is largely managed by the European Commission, while the politico-diplomatic choices related to the conflict remain in the hands of the EU member states. Furthermore, that logic has its history and even some output. Europe was advocating the right of self-determination of the Palestinians already back in 1980. It was a Danish and German initiative that led to the 2003 roadmap of the so-called "Quartet" on the Middle East (the United States, the UN, Russia, and the EU). More recently, with the Gaza Strip on the brink of a humanitarian crisis, it is the EU that has pushed for the creation of mechanisms to provide the Palestinians with emergency assistance and basic social support.

Worthy as they may be, the assets of the European policy are outweighed by its liabilities. Europe is routinely accused of having been misguided in its economic assistance to the Palestinian Authority. It is blamed for having limited its contribution to low-key, albeit important, initiatives (such as COPPS, an eponymously named mission assisting the reform of the Palestinian police). It has been criticized for fiddling on the side of the U.S. policy, and for its fragmentation.*

Pointedly, the candid report that UN Middle East Envoy Alvaro de Soto submitted upon his resignation in 2007 mentions the EU only a couple of times. And when it does, it is to say that, "Europeans have spent more money in boycotting the PA [Palestinian Authority] than they did when they were supporting it," that its border-monitoring mission between Gaza and Egypt (another of the EU's rather technical endeavors) was "fraught with difficulties," and that, "somewhat comically," the Quartet has, in fact, six members, since the EU is represented by three people.[14]

The Arab–Israeli conflict may be one of the causes—rather than the result—of Europe's record in the Mediterranean. However, if the EU receives such harsh bashing, it is because it has yet to deliver on its huge economic clout (residual), popularity among Arabs, and political potential. The Holy Land is high profile, but a similar assessment can arguably be adapted to other cases: from the precarious stalemate in Lebanon to the ossified conflict in the Western Sahara territory bordering Morocco.

At the heart of this underperformance is that Europe wrapped its misleading mythology of a single Mediterranean inside an equally misleading grand bargain. The EU has implied that freer trade and democratic reforms would reduce the gap between Europe and its southern partners. The problem here is not only that with such high

---

*In January 2009, as the international community was again scrabbling to stop the spiral of violence between Israel and Hamas in Gaza, the Czech Republic—holding the EU presidency—sent a diplomatic mission on behalf of the Union, several European governments placed the blame squarely on Hamas, and France condemned the Israeli offensive and put together a diplomatic mission of its own.

expectations, Europe's ineffectiveness counts much more; it is that there is no Cold War–style confrontation in the Mediterranean, let alone two interlocutors, and a détente cannot really be imposed by one party.

In the worst days of the occupation of Iraq, European diplomats were quite keen to privately remark that their modest framework was still wiser than "regime change." It has introduced a regional praxis of dialogue and consultation where previously there was none. The Southern Mediterranean states have not followed, Iran on a theocratic path.

All this is fine, except that the original plan was not damage control. Europe's "Barcelona Process" was about comprehensive political and economic reforms. It was about region-building, stability, and prosperity. On these counts, the harder truth is that with which a senior EU official (incidentally a Spaniard) dryly confronted a Brussels audience already some years ago: "Barcelona is dead."[15]

AN AWKWARD DEVOLUTION

Europe's reply to that somber verdict has apparently been, "Long live Barcelona." The EU policy remains in place, and all of the more recent initiatives in the region do not challenge its overall approach. That has been the fate of the EU's Neighborhood Policy in this region. This upgrades the existing agreements and specifies the terms of liberalization and market integration. Financial assistance is more generous and the sequencing of economic and political incentives more balanced. But this new policy neither replaces Europe's prevailing *modus operandi* nor fundamentally alters its logic.

The story of the new "Union for the Mediterranean" has been even unkinder. Nicolas Sarkozy attempted to bulldoze this new plan through the European debate even before his election as president. He envisioned something that would do for the Med what Jean Monnet did for Europe in the 1950s: a bold regional integration initiative of which "our children will be proud."[16]

That his charm offensive fell on deaf ears is not an exaggeration. European capitals either timidly endorsed or politely declined the scheme for at least three reasons: it was feared to disrupt the thin European foreign policy line, it was regarded as a substitute for Turkey's EU membership, and some even saw it as potentially competing with the EU itself. Characteristic of Europe's institutional overkill, since 2008 the Union for the Mediterranean has been embedded within the EU, upgrading and complementing the ongoing work in key sectors such as the environment, energy, research, and transportation. Its official name? "Barcelona Process: Union for the Mediterranean."

Although the dream of Euro-Mediterranean holism seems to remain alive for all intents and purposes, these more recent initiatives are, in reality, the product of what the EU's original policy has failed to deliver. The Union for the Mediterranean, diluted as it now is, remains aimed at addressing some of the more blatant shortcomings of the European regional approach. It has a secretariat in the region headed by two rotating consul-like figures (one from Europe and another from a North African country). While the initiative is open to all EU member states, policy-making is focused on the countries shoring the sea.

Similarly, the Neighborhood Policy is not quite the revolutionary breakthrough in EU methods that it was originally heralded as. But in the Southern Med, unlike Ukraine or Moldova or that aim for EU membership, the prospect of deeper market integration is probably as good as it gets and may well spark some reforms in countries such as Morocco and Jordan.

The trend is, then, in the direction of specialization and diversification: between what is done in Brussels, what can be accomplished by selected European countries, what is best tackled at the regional level, and what must be addressed by the North African and Middle Eastern countries themselves. This can explain the growing emphasis on the social and cultural aspects of the EU Med policy. It is illustrated by the repeated—if yet largely unheard—European calls for a more effective "South–South" cooperation, whose dim hopes presently rest on the moribund Arab-Maghreb Union and Agadir agreement.[17] A centrifugal shift is detectable in some diplomatic initiatives, such as the Spanish-Italian-French activism in brokering, in 2007, a domestic standoff in the fragmented political landscape of Lebanon. Similarly, 10 Southern European foreign ministers wrote an open letter in 2007 in which they asked Tony Blair, the former British Prime Minister and now representative of the Middle East Quartet, to put the redundant roadmap for peace out of its misery.[18]

Then there is migration, which, once again, is quite emblematic to capture the different layers of this picture. The free movement of people within the EU makes immigration a pan-European concern (and, indeed, provided Germany with a powerful argument against Sarkozy's Mediterranean Union plan). At the same time, it is an issue that has made necessary more focused coordination among European countries. The emergence of a "G-6" (France, Germany, Britain, Italy, Spain, and Poland) on illegal migration testifies to this.

And so does FRONTEX—the EU agency for border security—which coordinates selected countries on the patrol and control of the EU frontiers. Third, immigration requires the collaboration of North African governments. As key transit and immigration countries themselves, Libya and Morocco have thus entered bilateral—if often questionable—deals on migration with Italy and Spain, respectively.

As such, this kind of multileveled scheme is not the recipe for success, in the case of immigration, at least, not as long as Europe's position remains protective and its dominant discourse defensive. Yet, this differentiation resembles something that Europeans call "subsidiarity," a Catholic principle whereby policy-making ought to be delegated to the level of government that is closest to the individual.[19] In the Mediterranean, subsidiarity is not the product of any celestial design, and European initiatives remain tattered by an unwieldy blend of weighty rhetoric and scattergun implementation. Still, the point is that this labyrinth of overlapping initiatives does indicate the most likely destination of Europe's Mediterranean journey.

THE END OF THE MED AS WE KNOW IT?

"The sea, since it is as incapable of being seized as the air, cannot have been attached to the possessions of any particular nation." Thus wrote the 17th-century jurist Hugo Grotius in his aptly titled treatise *Mare Liberum* ("The Freedom of the Sea").[20] After having long regarded the Mediterranean as the most promising area to refute this claim, Europe now appears to be quietly resigning to it.

Evidently, the possessions that Europe might have wanted to claim in the Mediterranean are not territorial—not anymore. EU foreign policy planners must have known all along that the vision of unity embracing the whole region presented serious limitations. Yet, Europe has sought to build on its economic leverage to modernize, democratize, and even "Europeanize" its southern periphery. The EU has been careful never to spell out the latter ambition, thus shielding it both from the countries aspiring to the EU and from those that regard it as a neo-colonial anathema. But the EU's toolkit and mindset have, in practice, barely deviated from it. The European inability to bring about reforms in its southern periphery cannot be attributed to poor strategy alone. However, the domestic backlash in Europe has been more brutal than in other regions, and the Mediterranean region-in-the-making has turned into a nest of existential threats waiting to break into Europe.

The European outlook in the Mediterranean is not hopeless. European policy-makers have been aware all along that there is no such a thing as a single region encompassing the entire Mediterranean rim. The EU has become more responsive to the respective North African and Middle Eastern countries desiring closer ties to Europe. It has awakened to the unexpressed reform potential of civil society, and has reconciled with the notion that a handful of well-endowed projects is better than a lofty "Mediterranean Union."

That Europe may be refraining from dealing with the Mediterranean as a single region hardly seems an impressive feat. The United States, for one, has consistently steered clear of conflating the Middle East and North Africa into a single Mediterranean complex. Moreover, in Europe's case, the question—as always—concerns whether any such shift will translate into stronger engagement on the ground. The interesting twist here is precisely that the EU has not sanctioned any shift toward a different strategy in this region. In fact, Brussels has largely spared itself clashes over the grandeur of France's Mediterranean Union or the legacy of the Barcelona Process. The holistic markers of Europe's regional approach all remain bright and shiny.

What is changing is the substance: an intricate web of initiatives addressing the countries, policy areas, and different actors in the region. The real liberal deal is that countries, municipalities, firms, and non-governmental organizations find their optimal format of cooperation. No ambitious master plan is guiding this turn. But to the fading vision of a single Mediterranean region has corresponded a swell of initiatives with more targeted scope and attainable objectives.

Whether and how this move will change the way Europeans perceive the threats emanating from the South, and whether it will make a difference at all, remains to be seen. But the hidden moral may well be that the sooner Europe stops regarding its southern periphery as the chimerical "Mediterranean," the better equipped it will be to deal with its troubles.

7

The Wide West

When popular resentment against the United States has mounted during the best part of this decade, imperialism and hubris are charges that have resonated loudly in the regions of the European periphery just like in other corners of the globe. And yet think about the messianic welcome that George W. Bush received in Tirana, the capital of Albania, in 2007; about Bill Clinton Boulevard in Pristina, Kosovo; or about the Georgia Tbilisi International Airport, which greets travelers with Bush's crooked grin printed on a huge billboard. Even at the nadir of the reputation of the United States in the world, an American in search of comfort could find few places better than in some of the countries in this region.

This kind of reverence is reassuring, while, as 9/11 painfully taught, hatred can spiral into violence and tragedy in no time. Both sentiments, however, represent two sides of the same coin. They constitute a potent reminder that the United States remains the one player capable of mustering the power to sway the constellation of the wider European neighborhood.

Deep down, Europeans have always known this. They are aware that the EU global profile is still heavily influenced by the U.S. posture and by how Europe relates to it. The United States has played a role in many of their foreign policy ventures, whether by supporting them or by opting to steer clear of them.

This notwithstanding, throughout the Bush era, the European neighborhood—as much else—was simply nowhere to be found on the radar of the transatlantic relations. Europeans and Americans disagreed on the place that the westernmost former Soviet republics are to occupy in the Euroatlantic institutional setting. Political transformation in North Africa and the Middle East constituted one of the focal points of the post-Iraq clash between the two sides of the

Atlantic. Turkey's EU membership process has been all but frozen, and yet Bush's support for it was regarded as a "territory that isn't his" by former French President Jacques Chirac.

All that is meant to have changed now. The 200,000 Berliners that gathered in Tietgarten in July 2008 to meet then-Presidential candidate Barack Obama inaugurated a new transatlantic spring. Just as many European leaders studiously avoided associating themselves with the Bush administration, they fell over each other to congratulate the new President on his election. The United States and Europe are ready to rejoin forces to tackle the great challenges of our time.

Goodwill will no doubt help the two sides to address the substance of their respective approaches more candidly. But rapprochement also generates expectations, removes excuses, and places the onus on Americans and Europeans to act. The Bush-era hiatus had conveniently overshadowed a number of fundamental strategic differences, real policy inconsistencies, and serious implementation deficits across the Atlantic. The more the United States and Europe place their bitter divisions behind them, the more they will realize the scale of the challenge awaiting them.

A TALE OF TWO EUROPES

For a time during Bush's first term, the transatlantic debate was a dialogue among the deaf. The overwhelming military might displayed in the aftermath of 9/11 left Europe powerless in the face of Washington's choices. For their part, Europeans floundered in their endless quarrels about the merits of multilateralism. "Hard power and soft power," "Mars and Venus," "power and paradise" became the bestselling vocabulary depicting this division.[1] As the drama of post-war Iraq later unfolded and Europe's *schadenfreude* surfaced, the worldviews of the United States and Europe appeared to be drifting apart irreparably.

In retrospect, it seems particularly unfortunate that the bleakest phase of the "war on terror" happened to coincide with the peak of arrogance that some Europeans displayed with the EU's Eastern enlargement. For one, foreign policy orientations within Europe and the United States have never been as monolithic as this portrayal would suggest. Not all Europeans are incorrigible pacifists, and worldviews across the political spectrum in the United States can be just as diverse. Moreover, says the hard-core Atlanticist, the West is joined by a bond that is more resilient than a particular U.S. administration or a touchy European government would have it. Already in the 1950s, the North Atlantic area was envisaged as a space united by integration, sense of community, and joint expectations of peaceful change.[2] That cannot merely be a sign of token idealism. It testifies to the strength of the societal, political, and even moral ties across the Atlantic.

One of the most powerful symbols of this bond is what Timothy Garton Ash calls "the other 9/11": "European style, with the day before the month"—the fall of the Berlin Wall on November 9, 1989.[3] This 9/11 has not generated "shock and awe"; rather, it has concerned the creation of a Europe "whole and free."[4] A democratic and unified Europe constituted a paramount strategic guideline of the United States throughout the 1990s. This ambition was nurtured by political and diplomatic support. Economic aid and policy-specific support accompanied the transformation of post-communist countries. And it all made a perfect match with the EU enlargement process.

The expansion of the EU and NATO were thus mutually reinforcing in guiding the transition of Central Europe. However, analysts and policy-makers on both sides have probably undervalued the consequences of such a massive enlargement for the transatlantic relations and the European power constellation. The Atlantic discord in this sphere has rarely made the headlines. The subject is too nebulous to even make it to the bilateral agenda of U.S. and European leaders. But it is much deeper-rooted and more bipartisan than any of the Iraq-related squabbles.

On the one hand, we have seen that the European vision has become one in which this diverse region is dealt with in an increasingly differentiated manner. The successful policy of enlargement is giving way to an approach according to which neighbors are approached on a case-by-case basis and often without the offer of EU membership. The new Europe that is taking shape is not the result of a uniform and incremental expansion. It is the product of a more convoluted, and sometimes unintended, overlap of different layers of engagement. Enlargement remains in the cards for some countries, but the key European intuition of enhancing its collective security through regional integration is now being pursued by other, fuzzier means.

In contrast, the United States maintains a more definite approach. Washington has seen the enlargement of NATO and the EU as the primary tools to fulfill the vision of a united Europe. At the same time, U.S. policy has regarded the EU and NATO as playing different roles. EU integration is perceived as an ambitious economic project that has provided the tools to stabilize the continent and make it prosper, while NATO is entrusted with the task of ensuring security.

Americans have tended to underestimate the geopolitical implications of EU integration.[5] Washington does recognize the soft power of "Europeanization" in the absorptive—almost inertial—sense of the word. But it has downplayed the strategic implications of the widening of the EU, and has had reservations about considering the EU initiatives as a form of genuine foreign policy. Hence, where the prospect of further EU enlargement appears likely, as in the Balkans and Turkey, the United States has regarded Euroatlantic integration as an effective instrument for furthering its strategic goals in the region. In the absence of such prospects, U.S. policy is more likely to exit the sphere of Euroatlantic coordination.

This stylized depiction elicits a number of thoughts. A European observer could retort that the United States can afford a clearer posture, because it is not faced in this region with excruciating challenges, such as immigration and illegal smuggling. A more fitting comparison would be the relations between the United States and Latin American countries. A strategist could point out that the mindset of U.S. policy in areas such as the Middle East or Eastern Europe is driven by realpolitik rather than the inclusiveness and gradualism that is supposed to inspire the European policy-maker. Not incidentally, Russia regards the United States and NATO—not the EU—as its principal competitor on the European continent. A political theorist could further note that U.S. skepticism concerning the European approach dates all the way back to the question of sovereignty. The underlying assumption of the EU enlargement is that in order for the policy to work, a partner country agrees to entrust some of its powers to Brussels. For someone regarding state sovereignty as an inviolable prerogative, the question is to what extent a country can accept giving up part of its independence or, worse, believe that delegating power provides a solution to the challenges it faces.

These objections substantiate the argument that the emergence of a wider Europe has determined an unexpected impasse at the transatlantic level. In principle, much of the current European periphery ought to renew the historic venture of European reunification that was accomplished in the 1990s. Europeans and Americans agree about much more than they disagree in terms of values, priorities, and the means employed to attain them. Yet, the European neighborhood has turned into a symbolic frontline. Here, the United States and Europe display competing approaches to power. They project influence differently. Incompatible understandings on the figure of Europe are at play. The dust of the Iraq discord, one could argue, has quietly settled on the European periphery.

EU policy is more inconclusive. Europe's ability to persuade, attract, and transform its neighbors has not only an impact on the countries concerned, it carries consequences in the transatlantic context, too.

A NOT-SO-NEW BEGINNING

During the second half of the 1990s, nobody in Brussels or Washington ever really doubted that countries such as Poland, Hungary, or the Czech Republic belonged to Europe. Nobody in Europe questioned the commitment of the United States to ensuring the security of the continent and to supporting its reunification. Similarly, today nobody can reasonably object to the transformation of Ukraine into a prosperous democracy or that Turkey continues to modernize, while also preserving its internal stability.

Few, however, had predicted that the return of Central Europe to the European family would reopen the elusive questions that had hibernated throughout the four decades of the Cold War: where Europe ends and what Europe ultimately is. And few would have predicted that a taken-for-granted understanding of the goals could make Europe and the United States first complacent and then irritated at each other's approaches.

Today, Brussels and Washington can afford to be frank about one thing. With the partial exception of the troubled nations of the former Yugoslavia, the coordinated act of Euroatlantic integration as seen throughout the 1990s is over. Parallel NATO and EU membership are not in the cards for the rest of the former Soviet space or the Mediterranean area. Russia will seek to obstruct any maneuver that it deems provocative. The strategy of the synchronized expansion of NATO and the EU is not going to be replicated in any other country along the wider European periphery.

Because of the last enlargement round, the relations between NATO and the EU have also come under strain. After all, the dismal record of NATO–EU cooperation is, at least formally, motivated by one longstanding controversy in the European neighborhood: the Cyprus-Turkey conflict.[14] The strategic missions of the two Brussels organizations have also come to drift apart. NATO is aiming to transform itself into a security alliance with global aspirations and is set to engage ever more often in out-of-area missions such as Afghanistan (itself a key test for cooperation between Europeans and Americans). The EU, on the other hand, is seeking to deepen its institutional structure in order to define and strengthen its role as a political actor, including in the military field.

But asserting that Euroatlantic integration is no longer applicable in the same way as in Central Europe is not the same as saying that it is being shelved. The European backyard offers a number of valuable examples of how Euroatlantic integration is being reinvented. The Balkans is one of the few cases of moderately successful NATO–EU cooperation, at the strategic level as well as on the ground. This instance supports the claim that the transatlantic rapprochement in the European periphery represents a litmus test to the attractiveness of the Western alliance and to the credibility of both institutions.

Furthermore, the EU—rather than NATO—is assuming much of the responsibility for the military and civilian crisis management operations in the European neighborhood.[15] France's decision to rejoin NATO's command structures after more than 40 years and the evermore explicit U.S. recognition of the need of a strong European Security and Defence Policy further validate the promise of a more effective military coordination.

In the absence of a clear Euroatlantic perspective, both Europe and the United States are strengthening their engagement with the countries in the region by other means. Especially in Eastern Europe, EU and NATO policies do not appear tied to membership timetables. But they do provide the framework for focused work on the reforms that both institutions demand of these nations. In this realm, Russia has proven shrewd in highlighting the divisions between Europeans and Americans. If anything, the 2008 Georgia imbroglio has underscored the importance of a more consistent Western position in the relations with Moscow.

To allay the fears of new divisions on the continent, then, there are those constellations of countries willing to push for closer regional cooperation. The recent surge of European interest in the Black Sea region is complemented by U.S.-sponsored, private-public initiatives. The EU's Mediterranean architecture is paralleled by initiatives, such as the NATO Mediterranean Dialogue or, indeed, the Middle East Partnership Initiative. The least common denominator in these schemes is that regional cooperation constitutes the logical extension of the original European rationale of pooling resources, coordinating action, and building confidence through transnational cooperation.

Transatlantic cooperation also applies to themes and policy sectors of relevance. This is particularly the case with respect to energy, which represents a key interest for both European and the U.S. stakeholders in this part of the world. Policy-doers on both sides of the pond cannot but agree on the perils of their reliance, for both supply and transit, on many of Europe's unstable neighbors. NATO is mentioned time and again when it comes to the security of supplies.[16] Notwithstanding lower oil prices, Europe and the United States share an interest in enhancing their cooperation in terms of investment and of enforcement of existing legal and policy instruments. In an era when leaders on both sides are called upon to produce convincing answers on climate change, part of the limelight will fall on energy inefficiency and environmental predicament of many of the nations in this region.[17]

The wider European constellation has changed since the 2004 enlargements, and the transatlantic outlook has shifted with it. Neither of the measures mentioned here can replace the overarching Euroatlantic strategy of the 1990s, nor can they really match its compelling message. Yet, they do testify to the great, underexploited potential of transatlantic coordination.

One sure message to be drawn from the enthusiastic European rhetoric that greeted the election of Barack Obama is that the West, and the values that it embodies, cannot simply vanish. They will continue to elicit opposition, although also be an unparalled source of inspiration throughout the greater European continent. Renewed cooperation and even burden-sharing in the countries and regions of this area represents a natural focus to renew the transatlantic promise. It needs not be charged with expectations that can prove misleading. But the aspiration of a wider Europe, whole and free, should be valued for what it has always constituted: the finest accomplishment of the West.

Conclusion

A Sensible Europe

As Pope Benedict XVI, Joseph Ratzinger has not shied away from expressing his concerns about the future of Europe, Turkey's relations with it, and the threat of militant Islam. These concerns have not always been presented together, but have nevertheless ruffled a few feathers.[1] The distinguished theologian he is, Ratzinger has conveyed a more sophisticated message, though in no less stark terms. The West, and Europe in particular, he has argued, risk going toward "a dictatorship of relativism." "Recognizing nothing as definitive," Ratzinger has explained, relativism "leaves as the ultimate criterion only the self with its desires. And under the semblance of freedom it becomes a prison for each one, for it separates people from one another, locking each person into his or her own ego."[2]

This line of reasoning directly challenges the claim that the European mission is to contain seemingly incompatible cultural, religious, or ethnic instances and to wrap the continent in an ecumenical embrace of diversity. Europe's vaunted "difference" has overreached and plunged it into a deep existential crisis.

Whether or not one agrees with Pope Benedict, one thing stands clear. The European neighborhood is where this dilemma is being played out the most decisively. From Turkish EU aspirations to Russian bellicosity to immigration, the European backyard is the meeting place for fundamental dilemmas about what Europe is and aims to be as an organization, a foreign policy actor, and a polity.

This book has correlated the challenges arising from the periphery of the continent with the European governance structures, power constellation, and value system. In each case, it has arrived at one and the same conclusion: Europe cannot afford more inward-looking reflections as to what it is and what it wants to become. The European institutions, power, and identity are central to appreciating the neighborhood conundrum, though only if they elicit reflection concerning what Europe is capable of and willing to achieve. This means the rekindling of the European original nexus of security and integration—a task that is anything but relative.

OF FENCES AND NEIGHBORS

"Let us never forget, my friends, that Europe is a means and no end,"[3] stated Count Coudenhove-Kalergi in 1948, in his day one of the most visionary supporters of European integration. His warning still rings true. The prospect of an ever-enlarging Union has become a European fixation. Some regard it as a panacea to European troubles. For others, enlargement constitutes the paramount existential challenge to the European identity.

Both arguments are rooted in strong normative justifications, but they miss a central point. Wider European integration has proven conducive to fostering prosperity, spreading peace, and consolidating democracy throughout the continent. Nonetheless, the enlargement of the EU remains, first and foremost, a tool for achieving those goals, not the goal itself.

The endless internal quarrels are more about the expansion of the EU as a battlefield for the European soul than about a policy that is intended to accompany the political and economic transformation of the candidate countries; whether that transformation stalls or advances almost seems beside the point on occasion. This distortion is even more evident in relation to Europe's other neighbors from North Africa to Russia—countries that will probably never become part of the EU, and are not particularly bothered by that prospect. Here, the main concern in Europe is less about the rigor of its policies than about whether and how it can "Europeanize" these countries.

Let me be clear: The EU cannot shelve its enlargement policy just yet. The prospect for membership remains a powerful rationale to uphold the reform agenda of a partner country. The ambition of some of Europe's neighbors to join the EU is fully justified, especially if the EU has made an explicit promise. Europe must follow up on the pledge that it has made to the Balkans and it should welcome these nations into the Union as soon as they have fulfilled the conditions set out in the contract they all subscribed to. Shying away from the countless paradoxes characterizing the Turkish candidacy weakens Europe's standing; only by tackling them can Europe restore its credibility. The continuing domestic mayhem in Ukraine and Moldova hardly renders enlargement likely anytime soon; however, the EU ought to consider a long-term prospective membership for these two countries.

The argument here is precisely that it is first when Europe resolves the principled ambivalence about who is in and who is out that it will become possible to focus on the means at its disposal. The discussion about the political and geographical limits of Europe is fascinating, but if it overshadows what Europe is willing to do, it risks becoming futile. And remember, the European ambiguity regarding the former communist countries of Central Europe was constructive for the very reason that it was mostly about *when*—not *if*—they would eventually join the EU.

A shift of focus on the means will reveal that, in most policy-making domains, the path before Europe is largely laid out already. Despite the rantings of some populist politicians, the frontiers between the EU and its neighbors are timidly—almost secretly—opening. The average European may not be aware of it, but trade barriers are being lowered. If Europe is to free itself of its neighborhood angst, it must unmistakably continue in this direction.

Integration in the EU common market is a key tool to unleashing the reform potential in the neighboring countries. Economic integration, after all, remains the most enticing incentive for countries aiming at membership. "Deep" free trade arrangements, such as the one that was discussed in relation to Eastern Europe, will open up the EU market to selected neighbors. Non-tariff barriers and trade defenses are set to be lowered elsewhere in the European periphery. If the power of the attraction of the massive EU market is to be exploited to the full, the old European dream of a "Common European Economic Space" extending to the entire continent must become a reality.

The record of the single European foreign policy is too thin to discern a long-term pattern, but integration is being pursued in this field as well. Ukraine and Moldova, for example, have subscribed to over 95 percent of the EU foreign policy declarations in recent years. Morocco contributed troops to the EU peacekeeping forces in Bosnia; Ukraine itself has sent personnel to EU police missions in the Balkans. The EU member states guard their foreign policy prerogatives so jealously that it is difficult to imagine any of the neighbors gaining a stake in EU decision making in this field. But the geographical position and the historical and cultural backgrounds of some of these countries are invaluable assets in specific contexts. Europe can only benefit from their gradual inclusion in the EU foreign policy machinery.

Then there is the most sensitive domain of all: what the EU somewhat misleadingly refers to as "movement of people." People coming from the European backyard are not "moving" nearly enough
for anyone's good. They are either stuck in lengthy and degrading
queues in European consulates, or risk their necks trying to sneak illegally through the European border. And when they get into the EU,
many are led to live in a sort of preventive social probation.

A part of the European subconscious seems to operate on the
assumption that immigration may or should at some point cease altogether. That attitude is not viable and Europe is very slowly coming to
terms with it. The EU has launched a "blue card" program to attract
skilled migrants, visa liberalization is the name of the game in the Balkans, and visa-facilitation deals are underway in Eastern Europe. The
rationale behind these moves is plain. A long queue at the consulate
does not deter the ruthless human-trafficker, but it does scare away
the motivated and entrepreneurial migrant craved by Europe. The
choice cannot be one in which Europe either opens its borders com-
pletely or seals them. In the long run, the only plausible outcome of
this painstaking process must be visa-free travel for the EU candidate
countries and the more advanced non-candidates.

For all of this to happen, the *sine qua non* is the same as usual.
Europe will have to be firm and crystal clear about its conditions. The
EU market will only open up in return for the approximation of the
neighboring country's regulatory framework to EU standards. Foreign
policy dialogue requires a track record in the partner country that
demonstrates respect for human rights and democratic principles—
both at home and abroad. Immigration procedures can be relaxed if
the neighbors take responsibility for their own migration policy.
Under these circumstances, some neighbors are likely to remain pari-
ahs. But the incentives will encourage the more ambitious ones to
push through tough legislation and comprehensive reforms.

With these measures in place, some neighbors may be confronted
with a startling discovery. The difference between the category of EU
member and that of partner with the EU blurs to the point of indis-
tinction. Some neighbors, like Turkey, will have to swallow a restric-
tive EU accession deal consisting of exceptions and "safeguards." But
for a country such as Israel, whose market is deeply integrated with
the EU and whose citizens can already travel freely to Europe, the
question of EU membership has long been redundant.

Enlargement remains an effective European policy and, in a country like Ukraine, its political and symbolic value is bound to remain
the most significant incentive the EU can offer. In the future, however, if some country will question whether the enlargement process

is all worth it, it will not necessarily be because Europe is hopelessly hesitant or its neighbors perpetually unstable. It will be because both have other means to pursue their common goals.

THE CONTINENT'S CONSTELLATIONS

Were we to do all of the above, the Euro-purist might argue, the EU would fragment beyond repair. The wider European neighborhood would become a maze of country-specific agreements and confusing acronyms. Decision-making capabilities will weaken and Europe will lose its remaining coherence.

Here are two counterarguments. First, Europe is *already* a maze of specific agreements and confusing acronyms. Ireland and Britain are not part of the so-called "Schengen area" of free movement of persons, while Switzerland, which is not an EU member, has joined it. A country like Norway has chosen to stay out of the EU altogether, although it is part of a framework called the European Economic Area (EEA), through which it is largely included in the EU single market. In contrast, Turkey and, after the financial meltdown of 2008, may be even Iceland, are seeking EU membership, but they are already a member of things like the European Environmental Agency (also EEA), one of the specialized EU bodies. Differentiation is not terribly new in Europe; if anything, it is bound to increase as the EU enlarges.

Second, if Euro-purists hope to counter this trend by attempting to include all of these differences within the EU framework, then disintegration might well become a self-fulfilling prophecy. The succession of impenetrable EU treaties was made necessary to streamline EU decision-making procedures. But the attempt to fit everything into the EU has effectively sunk Europe into a state of permanent negotiations. Revealingly, the EU would even provide for a smaller number of member countries to "enhance cooperation" in selected sectors, though the fact that this provision has never been applied testifies to the paralysis of the Union.

Instead, the European countries join together in smaller groups *outside* of the EU context. I already mentioned the cooperation among six EU countries (G-6) on immigration, to which one can add the cooperation among Britain, France, Germany, Spain, and Italy on counter-terrorism. It might appear as though the bigger and more ambitious countries, feeling constrained by the EU, resolve to do without it.

But similar arrangements actually have a long and glorious history throughout Europe, regardless of the size or geographical position of a given country. From the Nordic cooperation to the seven signatories of the so-called Treaty of Prüm on internal security; from the Visegrad Group (Hungary, Poland, Slovakia, and the Czech Republic) all the way back to the Benelux, the political map of Europe has never quite been as orderly as the EU treaties would imply. It looks more like a bowl of noodles consisting of innumerable regional, multileveled, or sector-specific arrangements.[4] The origins and purpose of these configurations vary greatly, from linguistic and cultural ties to common economic or political interests. But the broader point is that these overlapping formations are not a sacrilege to the European orthodoxy; they constitute its very essence, just as the laws emanating from Brussels.

The relevance of these constellations for Europe's neighbors cannot be overestimated. It is as natural for Poland to reach out to Ukraine as it is for Romania to develop ties with Moldova. In the Mediterranean, Baltic, and Black Seas, dreams of regional unity have possibly been exaggerated. But the countries shoring these basins share much in terms of challenges and opportunities, whether or not they are EU member states.

A similar point applies to European foreign and security policy. The EU foreign policy will gain some coherence if and when the Reform Treaty will enter into force, and the Union will at long last have a full-time President as well as a Foreign Minister and a Foreign Service in everything but name. Even so, the international activism of varying collections of countries has already demonstrated the European potential. Selected European states have, in practice, represented Europe, from the Balkans (within the so-called "Contact Group") to Iran (Britain, Germany, and France—the "EU3") and may continue to do so in particularly sensitive theaters such as the Middle East—with or without an EU Foreign Minister.

These configurations may even go some way towards solving one of the most serious dilemmas of contemporary European integration: defense cooperation, including the EU contribution to conflict resolution and mitigation. Peacekeeping operations, such as the one that followed the 2006 conflict between Hezbollah and Israel in Lebanon, do not carry an EU label. Nonetheless, that mission remains eminently "European," quite simply because it would not have been possible without the substantial involvement of European countries. If the EU wants to be taken seriously in the international arena, it must find a way to flex its military muscle. And if it is to flex it effectively, it will have to come up with "pioneer groups" such as the one that ventured to Lebanon.[5]

Perhaps most peculiarly, this phenomenon has moved beyond—or rather beneath—the state level in the form of cross-border interaction among municipalities, non-governmental actors, and firms. Town twinnings, itinerant cultural events, and "Euro-regions" extend beyond the border between Europe and its neighbors—making it more porous and less rigid.

If one wonders what a town twinning in the remote outskirts of Europe has got to do with the strategic future of a continent, one should consider this. In May 2007, the bilateral relations between the EU and Russia were at one of the lowest points. As European and Russian leaders met for one of their regular summits, Moscow had serious bilateral disputes with several countries, including neighboring Poland, Lithuania, and Estonia. The Russian police were detaining undesired demonstrators, and Germany's Angela Merkel, representing the EU on that occasion, openly criticized the Kremlin. The parties were so at odds that they did not manage (or maybe, more wisely, declined) to formulate one of their joint statements about "common values."

At that very same meeting, however, Moscow pledged an unprecedented €200 million ($266 million) for cross-border cooperation with the EU.[6] In a climate that was worryingly reminiscent of the Cold War, Moscow proposed to spur exchanges among people and local authorities in the common EU-Russian periphery. Among the beneficiaries of these exchanges would be countries such as Poland, Lithuania, and Estonia.

Europeans remain too divided—even naïve—about Russia's foreign policy posturing, and Russia has cashed in on wishful European thinking. Nevertheless, if the EU insists on engaging Russia rather than merely buying its gas and hoping for the best, it is also because of gestures such as this one.

Those concerned about the growing diversity within Europe can sleep easy. These constellations are not going to turn the wider Europe into a nightmare of loose, overlapping agreements. On the contrary, they complement what is being done in Brussels. Regional cooperation gives meaning to the treasured European reference to the "joint ownership" of policies and processes. From multilateral diplomacy to cooperation among small villages, this is all evidence of Europe's resources and capabilities. At a time of European self-examination, such as the present, these constellations preserve the spirit of inclusion and shared sovereignty upon which the EU is founded. And as Europe grows more diverse, they actually reinforce that spirit.

On at least one count, however, the Euro-purists have a point. Diversity can dilute the core message that Europe is meant to convey. The considerations inspiring the Italian government in its energy deals with Russia are different from those guiding the strenuous Polish opposition to Moscow. The values driving the support of the British government to the Turkish EU bid clash with those accounting for the Austrian opposition to it. Ideological divergence regarding the future of Europe and disagreements over policy provides a great deal of explanation concerning these inconsistencies. However, they do not answer the question as to what Europe is actually supposed to be promoting in its backyard.

THE PARTS AND THE WHOLE

By now, it is probably safe to say that few Europeans bought into George W. Bush's "freedom agenda." For their own particular reasons, some European countries went along with the administration's rhetoric on the promotion of democracy and its axiomatic association with the war on terrorism. But all of them most likely welcome a return of the United States to the more gradualist and composite posture, which the political scientist Francis Fukuyama now refers to as "new democratic realism."[7]

Europe, to be sure, has its own axioms concerning the promotion of democracy. In what would make a good slogan for democratic peace theory, the European Security Strategy recites that, "the best protection for our security is a world of well-governed democratic states." The pull of the EU enlargement process has proven one of the most successful exercises of democracy promotion in modern history. Europeans have their own "freedom agenda," and the correlation between security and integration is at the heart of it.

When integration and security are taken separately, however, it seems that Europe loses much of its democratic passion. Concerning integration, the EU is an institution that is respected for its accountability, though not always for its democratic legitimacy.[8] When the citizens of Europe vote against the EU in popular referenda, some of their governments get them to vote again until they produce the "right" result. On many key strategic issues, the EU is still governed by a system of unanimity that renders negotiations into an exhausting, intergovernmental bazaar.

Abroad, the EU common instruments purely devoted to promoting democracy are somewhat modest in size and scope. Strategic and economic considerations divide the European countries as to what to promote. And that is not to mention the differences in how this is being carried out. To cite but one comparison: Sweden spends an estimated 24 percent of its development assistance budget on democracy-related initiatives; the figure for France is a mere 1 percent.[9]

The European democracy agenda in its periphery may not be as poor and weak as is sometimes portrayed but it is quite contradictory. The European focus on state building in the Balkans has been something of a necessity dictated by the regional post-conflict predicament. In Eastern Europe, the EU's efforts have concentrated on poor governance and promoting institutions. Economic development has remained the priority in North Africa and the Middle East.

There is nothing wrong with any of these measures. On the contrary, institutional capacity, the rule of law, and economic development are all crucial pillars for a sustainable democratic process. Furthermore, the European focus is a healthy reaction to the assumption that any country moving *away* from autocracy is inevitably in transition *toward* democracy. The Soviet Union collapsed almost two decades ago; Hosni Mubarak has been President of Egypt for 30 years; Muammar Qaddafi has led Libya for 40. Many of the European neighbors are not exactly "in transition" to anywhere, and a different approach is worth trying.

Nevertheless, Europe may have fallen into the opposite trap.[10] Support for functioning state institutions do not necessarily come before—and cannot replace—the development of a full-fledged liberal democracy. The events surrounding the 2004 Orange Revolution in Ukraine illustrate this best. EU top officials, even the presidents of Poland and Lithuania, proved reactive at the time in defusing the brewing crisis. Their engagement was instrumental to brokering an agreement between the opposing parties about a repetition of the run-off presidential election. That election marked Viktor Yushchenko's triumph and the high point of his bloodless revolution.

Yet, all that Brussels was able to offer after these outstanding events was a 10-point update of a bilateral "Action Plan" that had been negotiated by Yushchenko's predecessor and adversary. And ever since the revolution, Europe has sought to step up its governance assistance to Ukraine. But it has not properly accounted for the fact that the Orange revolutionaries have since twice dissolved their governing coalition and plunged the country into four years of political chaos. Brokering a deal between two contenders does not mean that a civic revolution can be all but ignored. The advancement of governance standards does not compensate for an ungovernable country. These preconditions of democracy are a complement to, not a surrogate of, a focus on things such as fair political competition.

In other words, Europe needs its own dose of new democratic realism—but of the opposite sort of what Fukuyama recommends for the United States. The European approach must also be gradualist, though in the sense that it should build on what it is already doing in order to define a more comprehensive democracy strategy. This means that support for tax reforms or privatization programs ought to be reinforced by a more effective assistance to civil society and the development of political parties.

If this support is to match developments on the ground, the EU should strive to spell out the full array of conditions aimed at improving the state of democracy in partner countries. It needs to get tougher and stricter concerning the negative consequences that countries will face if they backtrack on their commitments. The continuum of incentives and penalties should be country-specific and comprehensive; it should provide for the kind of platform where the European and U.S. approaches can converge.

Above all, foreign powers can support and assist the advancement of democracy, though that democracy must ultimately emerge and develop on the ground. Europeans and Americans alike must be reminded about that, albeit for the opposite reasons.

INTO THE RELATIVE ORDER OF THE WORLD

In the epigraph that opens this book, Dante Alighieri talks about— or rather to—his beloved Florence. Like the Italian city-state in the 13th and 14th century, post-war Europe has been incessantly renewing its "customs, and laws, and coins, and offices." Not unlike Dante's Florence, it is no stretch to argue that Europe is often regarded as a "sick wretch," whose contortions reveal a fragility that is particularly evident when examining the bloc's foreign policy aspirations.

In recent years, the question of the relative decline of the United States' world primacy has made it to the center of the debate in international affairs. The decline is relative, because the United States is bound to remain, at least for the foreseeable future, the preeminent global power. At the same time, this decline has not generated what some Europeans used to perceive as a "multipolar" world order consisting of different centers of global attraction catching up and then competing equally with the United States. Rather, it is characterized by the emergence of what some have called "relative" powers.[11]

Regional players such as Russia, China, India, and Brazil have found their place among the relative powers. More traditional players such as the UN or the World Trade Organization still provide inclusive, albeit not always functional, forums for global dialogue. Non-governmental organizations, such as Greenpeace, and philanthropic bodies, such as the Gates Foundation, have made their way into the global agenda. And then come multinational corporations, media conglomerates, terrorist networks; the world's relative powers come in multiple shapes, some of them unthinkable merely a few years ago.

These actors are not necessarily "relative" in terms of what they stand for—in some cases, like Al Qaeda, they hold on to rather absolute values. Their rise is a relative phenomenon in the sense that some of them may pose a serious challenge to the United States in some field but none of them is likely to supplant the United States' political, economic, or military might and attractiveness and emerge as the sole superpower of the 21st century.

This shifting configuration has been labeled in different ways,[12] and more debate can only be expected in the years to come. For the sake of clarity, I am sticking with "neo-medieval." This does not mean that the global clock will turn back to what historian Niall Ferguson calls a new Dark Age: "an era of waning empires and religious fanaticism; of endemic plunder and pillage in the world's forgotten regions; of economic stagnation and civilization's retreat into a few fortified enclaves."[13] Many of the new powers represent the most notable products of globalization. A new Dark Age would be one in which not only the United States' power shrinks; according to this view, it would be an era in which globalization utterly reverses.

Still, an order characterized by the United States' diminishing global reach and by different kinds of emerging powers does in some respects resemble the state of affairs of Dante's age. His was a world in which the general pattern of Western Christendom was in practice characterized by a plethora of deeply interwoven, and increasingly influential, power players. The result was an international environment in which alliances were made and broken, cooperation could quickly turn into competition; it was a system that remained interconnected, somewhat structured, but also extremely fluid.

How and where does today's Europe fit in such an order? Europe itself, you may recall, is supposed to be neo-medieval: its sovereignty shared, political authority diffused, and borders fuzzy. But in the one place in which all of this is supposed to happen today, in Europe's backyard, it is only happening very slowly. If Europe is not to sink into this uncertain global constellation, it will have to renew the ways, places, and niches in which its positions are valued and its value recognized. It will have to be ambitious about what it can do and realistic about what it cannot. In addition to being key to Europe's own sustainability, a sensible strategy for the broader neighborhood represents the ultimate frontline of Europe's global vision.

The goal of a rule-based world shaped by norms also promoted by Europe has already made considerable advances. Europe is the recognized global leader in the field of environmental regulations and standards. Contravening EU competition laws may end up being very costly for non-compliant corporations, as Microsoft and General Electric well know. The "precautionary principle" underpins the EU legislation requiring industry to demonstrate in advance that products do not pose environmental or health-related hazards.[14] Producers worldwide comply with these regulations in order to sell their products in the European market.

Notwithstanding these impressive achievements, Brussels' regulatory power struggles in relation to its backyard. The adoption and implementation of EU economic rules on the part of Europe's neighbors is patchy at best. Quite arbitrarily, regulation means liberalization for some countries and protectionism for others, not to mention Gazprom's *ad libitum* interventions in the European energy market. If the EU does not manage to extend its influence evenly in its own backyard, the title of the world's leading regulator will have lost some of its luster.

Europhiles also argue that the vision of a globe arranged in regional groupings modeled on the image of Europe is already coming true in the shape of the African Union, ASEAN (in Southeast Asia), and Mercosur (in Latin America).[15] This may be true, but the process leading to these organizations is hardly comparable with the post-world war circumstances behind European integration.

Regionalism in these other areas has done little to alleviate endemic poverty, income inequalities, authoritarianism, open conflicts, or ethnic cleansing. The African Union and ASEAN have in their ranks members such as Zimbabwe and Myanmar (formerly Burma), whose political standards would never qualify for EU membership. In many ways, regionalism in the developing world has paid lip service to the European model. But it neither resembles it nor has it been conducive to a betterment of the economic and political predicaments in these other regions.

If Europe can be of concrete inspiration to these regions, it will be also because it shows how to deal with the non-democratic regimes in its own neighborhood. European regionalism can provide a model for Africa if it manages to solve its own conflicts in the Caucasus and the Balkans (while also lending a hand in Chad or Sudan). Latin American countries have not adopted an accumulated rulebook comparable to the EU *acquis communautaire.* But most of Europe's neighbors have not adopted it, either. What the EU relies upon in these cases is a corpus consisting of multilateral conventions, treaties and declarations to which both EU members and its neighbors have subscribed. If Europe can, indeed, be a model for regional development worldwide, it is also to the extent that it will be able to tackle comparable challenges. For Europe, these challenges coalesce in its own periphery.

Europeans may have had to sideline "multipolarity" as the final destination of their global journey but they have not given up on their preferred recipe to run the world. They have not abandoned the conviction that the actors on the world stage ought to strive for inclusive solutions to common concerns. They continue to believe that any player who has a stake in the global development—from the cardiologist volunteering in a developing country to the occupant of the White House—also has a responsibility.

It could all be discarded as insufferable idealism but Europeans cannot really think any differently. Ever-deeper cooperation is the way in which Europeans have found peace. The inclusion of an ever-greater number of stakeholders is the way in which peace in Europe has been nurtured. Integration is not simply a strategic choice, it represents the European way of life.

If the European approach to democracy promotion, economic development, and conflict-resolution will work in the troubled regions of its backyard, Europe will be able to claim that integration continues to provide an important tool to navigate this uncertain world. If the European approach will not work there, what will fail is not only a model of governance, it will be nothing less than the failure of a way of life.

Acknowledgments

From Ankara to Zagreb, dozens of people across three continents have made it possible for this book to come to fruition. First, I would like to thank the three research institutions that have hosted me while this project was in the making. The Department of Political Science at the University of Copenhagen has provided the physical and intellectual base to which I could return after my journeys across the European periphery: other globetrotters will agree that this is much more than just a logistical detail. I thank the Department leadership for granting me a sabbatical leave in the fall of 2007 to work on this book, as well as the University's research priority area "Europe in Change," which funded fieldwork and editorial assistance. I have been privileged to share my ideas with over 300 students coming from every corner of the world who have followed my courses in recent years. After being lectured about it for months, some of them may not get to read these pages, but I thank them nevertheless.

Madeleine Albright once argued that "to understand Europe, you have to be a genius—or French." In my mind, it wouldn't hurt to also pass by the Centre for European Policy Studies (CEPS) in Brussels. I am grateful to its research and support staff for the hospitality, and to Director Daniel Gros for our lively, though often depressing, discussions on Italian politics and economy. The Riksbanken Jubileumsfond of Sweden has generously funded much of my research at CEPS. Special thanks to Michael Emerson, the head of the CEPS unit on EU foreign and security policy. When it comes to European integration issues, he is one of the few people I know who is not only gifted with the ability to master the big strategic picture and the smallest policy details; he is also brilliant when it comes to putting them together.

The Center for Transatlantic Relations at the Johns Hopkins' School of Advanced International Studies (SAIS) in Washington, DC has been carrying out first-class research on Europe. I dare say that the accomplishments of Center Director Dan Hamilton, Director of Research Esther Brimmer and their staff in studying and communicating Europe in the United States are of almost Tocquevillian proportions. I thank them, as well as Katrien Maes and Gretchen Losee, for their kindness and support.

Many analysts, activists, diplomats, and civil servants have shared their ideas, commented on my writings, or encouraged me at one stage or another. Understandably, some of them wish to remain anonymous. Of the others, I wish to thank Noel Parker, Geoffrey Edwards, and Pertti Joenniemi regarding the more conceptual parts of this book; Orlando Fusco, Jovan Teokarevic, Ivan Barbalic, Danijel Pantic, Predrag Vujicic, Maja Kovacevic, Hedvig Morvai Horvath, and Vlatko Sekulovic on the Balkans; Senem Aydin, Alain Servantie, Mustafa Aydin, and Özgür Özdamar on Turkey; Nicu Popescu, Arkady Moshes, Marius Vahl, Lars Grønbjerg, and Sergiu Celac on Eastern Europe and Russia; Gianni Bonvicini, Antonio Missiroli, Rosa Balfour, and Nathalie Tocci on North Africa and the Middle East; Steve Larrabee, Ian Lesser, Mike Haltzel, and Ed Joseph on U.S. policy.

Michael Calingaert and Dennis Redmont of the Council of the United States and Italy have put together an outstanding group of young leaders from both sides of the Atlantic, from which I have drawn much inspiration. John Sitilides and Andri Peros have twice offered me a podium at the Woodrow Wilson International Center for Scholars in Washington, DC from where I could present my ideas. They didn't know this until now, but the title of this book occurred to me in a room that they reserved in a very suggestive Washington hotel. Janos Herman at the European Commission has provided me with a wealth of contacts and insights and is generously endowed with what I believe is a quintessential quality for a diplomat: listening. Thanks to Jon Jay Neufeld, for his editorial skills and for his friendship. Robert Hutchinson at Praeger has been patient, flexible, and open-minded beyond my expectations. None of these outstanding individuals, of course, are responsible for what you may read in this book.

Those closest to me, my family and friends in Rome and Copenhagen, have tolerated my long disappearances; more than that, they have tolerated my last-minute appearances and provided hospitality above and beyond the call of duty. To my delight, they have all been genuinely curious about the details of this book. My brother, Mirko, possibly provided the most unambiguous go-ahead after reading one of the chapters and commenting: "It's got to do with us here in Europe."

My utmost gratitude goes to Marie, who saw this book coming long before it was ever conceived, and to William, to whom the book is dedicated. He will not be able to read it for quite some years yet, but that is exactly how it is supposed to be: to paraphrase Nietzsche, there is nothing more serious than a child at play.

Notes

I have refrained from turning this section into a "bibliographic genealogy." These notes are only meant to give reference to facts and quotations, and to indicate where I have relied directly on a secondary source for insight. In those instances where a series of facts draws on different sources, only one superscript note is inserted at the end of the paragraph. Internet links change all the time, and I have cited only the homepage where the information was originally found. All U.S. dollar equivalents to original Euro figures are based on mid-April 2009 exchange rates.

Introduction: Thy Neighbor, Thyself

1. The figures are from: *World Migration 2008: Managing Labour Mobility in the Evolving Global Economy* (Geneva: International Organization for Migration, 2008), 455 and 466.

2. The country-by-country conservative estimates of the Geneva-based Internal Displacement Monitoring Centre add up to over 3 million internally displaced persons in the countries surrounding the EU. The World Refugee Survey published by the U.S. Committee for Refugees and Immigrants in 2008 estimates about 3 million refugees or asylum seekers in the region. See http://www.internal-displacement.org and http://www.refugees.org.

3. The figures on Islam and the West are from a 2008 Gallup poll published by the World Economic Forum, *Islam and the West: Annual Report on the State of Dialogue* (Geneva: World Economic Forum, 2008), 25. The figures on Russia and Turkey are from the German Marshall Fund and Compagnia di San Paolo, *Transatlantic Trends: Key Findings* (2008), 21.

4. Charlemagne, "How Terrorism Trumped Federalism," *The Economist*, October 2, 2004.

5. Robert Cooper, *The Breaking of Nations: Order and Chaos in the Twenty-First Century*. (London: Atlantic Books, 2003), 138.

6. "A Secure Europe in a Better World," *European Security Strategy*, Brussels, December 12, 2003, 8.

7. These two contrasting positions have been put forward most provocatively by Robert Kagan, *Of Paradise and Power: America and Europe in the New World Order* (London: Atlantic Books, 2003) and by Mark Leonard, *Why Europe will Run the 21st Century* (London: 4th Estate, 2005).

8. Daniel Hamilton and Joseph Quinlan, *Globalization and Europe: Prospering in the New Whirled Order* (Washington, D.C.: Center for Transatlantic Relations, Johns Hopkins University, 2008), 59–70. See also World Bank, "Europe and Central Asia" and "The Middle East and North Africa" *World Development Indicators*, Fact sheets, 2007, retrievable at http://www.worldbank.com.

9. Most explicitly, R.B.J. Walker, "Europe Is Not Where It Is Supposed to Be," in *International Relations Theory and the Politics of European Integration: Power, Security and Community*, ed. Morten Kelstrup and Michael Williams (London: Routledge, 2000).

Chapter 1: Where Europe Is Not

1. The context provided here draws on Geo Widengren, *Mani and Manichaeism* (London: Weidenfeld and Nicolson, 1961).

2. The commentary was published simultaneously in Germany and France. Jürgen Habermas and Jacques Derrida, "Europe: Plaidoyer Pour Une Politique Extérieure Commune," *Liberation* and "Nach dem Krieg: Die Wiedergeburt Europas," *Frankfurter Allgemeine Zeitung*, May 31, 2003. An English version was later published as "February 15, or, What Binds Europeans Together: A Plea for a Common Foreign Policy Beginning in the Core of Europe," in *Old Europe, New Europe, Core Europe: Transatlantic Relations after the Iraq War*, ed. Daniel Levy, Max Pensky, and John Torpey (London: Verso, 2005).

3. Iver B. Neumann has explored this question at length and always with very inspiring results. See his, "Self and Other in International Relations," *European Journal of International Relations* 2/2 (1996).

4. Ole Wæver has put forward the most persuasive exposition of this point. See his "European Security Identities," *Journal of Common Market Studies* 34/1 (1996).

5. *Economic Growth in Europe since 1945*, eds. Nicholas Crafts and Gianni Toniolo (Cambridge: Cambridge University Press, 1996).

6. Timothy Garton Ash, "Europe's True Stories," *Prospect* 131 (February 2007).

7. For this quote, and a good summary of the role of the Marshall Plan in the European integration process, Christiane Höln, "Truman's Marshall Plan—A Lesson in Leadership," *European Voice*, June 12, 2008.

8. Andrew Moravcsik, "Negotiating the Single European Act: National Interests and Conventional Statecraft in the European Community," *International Organization* 45/1 (Winter 1991).

9. The first quote is from Francis Fukuyama: "The End of History?" in *The National Interest* (Summer 1989), 4. The second is by John J. Mearsheimer, "Back to the Future: Instability in Europe after the Cold War," *International Security* 15/1 (1990), 6.

10. See, for example, *The Idea of Europe: from Antiquity to the European Union*, ed. Anthony Pagden (Cambridge: Cambridge University Press, 2002).

11. As German Finance Minister Peer Steinbrück made sure to remark during the subprime-triggered financial crisis that started in 2008, laissez-faire was "as simplistic as it was dangerous." Similar comments were made by German Chancellor Angela Merkel and French President Nicolas Sarkozy. For good measure, key Republican figures in the United States have warned that President Obama's 2009 budget risked tilting the U.S. economy in a "European socialist" direction.

12. Tony Judt, *Postwar: A History of Europe since 1945* (London: William Heinemann, 2005), 73 and 77.

13. Habermas and Derrida, "February 15, or . . .", 10.

14. Political scientist Joseph Nye famously defined this quality as "soft power." This notion is explained in his *Soft Power: The Means to Success in World Politics* (New York: Public Affairs, 2004).

15. Derrida is himself the philosopher who has thought most thoroughly about this. See his *The Other Heading: Reflections on Today's Europe* (Bloomington: Indiana University Press, 1992).

16. Jeremy Rifkin, *The European Dream: How Europe's Vision of the Future Is Quietly Eclipsing the American Dream* (Cambridge: Polity Press, 2005).

17. Albert Camus, *Resistance, Rebellion, and Death* (New York: Alfred A. Knopf, 1961), 243.

18. Jan Zielonka has spelled out the most exhaustive application of this argument in his *Europe as Empire: The Nature of the Enlarged European Union* (Oxford: Oxford University Press, 2006). The earliest statement on the argument, however, belongs to Ole Wæver, "Europe's Three Empires: A Watsonian Interpretation of Post-Wall European Security" in *International Society after the Cold War: Anarchy and Order Reconsidered*, ed. Rick Fawn and Jeremy Larkins (London: MacMillan Press, 1996).

19. Quoted in Robert Cooper: *The Breaking of Nations . . .* , 78.

20. Ulrich Sedelmeier and Frank Schimmelfennig "Governance by Conditionality: EU Rule Transfer to the Candidate Countries of Central and Eastern Europe," *Journal of European Public Policy* 11/4 (2004).

21. Jan Zielonka, *Europe as Empire . . .* , 167.

22. This is part of what Ian Manners calls "normative power." "Normative Power Europe: A Contradiction in Terms?" *Journal of Common Market Studies* 40/2 (2002).

23. Francesco Giavazzi and Alberto Alesina, *The Future of Europe: Reform or Decline* (Cambridge: MIT Press, 2006), 5. The figures cited in this section refer to Western Europe and are drawn from this accessible study on the state and prospects of the European economy.

24. Richard Lambert and Nick Butler, *The Future of European Universities: Renaissance or Decay?* (London: Centre for European Reform, 2006).

25. For this argument, Nicholas Eberstadt and Hans Groth, "Healthy Old Europe" in *Foreign Affairs* 86 (May/June 2007). See also Eurostat, *Newsrelease*, 119/2008, August 26, 2008.

26. The Common Agricultural Policy eats up some 40 percent of the EU's budget while producing about 2 percent of its GDP.

27. This data is from Eurobarometer, Public Opinion in the European Union 69: First Results, Brussels, June 2008, 20–21.

28. EU Enlargement Commissioner Olli Rehn in Alison Smale and Dan Bilefsky, "Fighting EU 'Enlargement Fatigue,' " *International Herald Tribune* June 20, 2006.

29. The myth is recalled in Zygmunt Bauman's poetic pamphlet *Europe: An Unfinished Adventure* (London: Polity, 2004).

30. This is an argument that my colleagues Michael Emerson, Senem Aydin, Julia de Clerck Sachsse, and Gergana Noutcheva have meticulously demonstrated in their "Just What Is This Absorption Capacity of the European Union?" *CEPS Policy Brief* 113 (2006). In a May 2008 *Eurobarometer* survey, only 28 percent of the population in Germany, 32 in France, and 36 in the United Kingdom supported the further enlargement of the EU.

31. European Council, *Presidency Conclusions* (Brussels: June 21–22, 2007), 12.

32. EU External Relations Commissioner Benita Ferrero Waldner as quoted by Michael Emerson (ed.) *Democratisation in the European Neighbourhood* (Brussels, CEPS Paperbacks, 2005), 215.

Chapter 2: The Path to Normalcy

1. I have heard this sentence from Haris Silajdzic, a member of the tripartite Presidency of Bosnia, at a meeting at the Johns Hopkins School of Advanced International Studies, Washington, D.C., November 9, 2007.

2. Warren Zimmermann, *Origins of a Catastrophe: Yugoslavia and Its Destroyers* (New York: Times Books, 1996), vii.

3. Maria Todorova has vigorously criticized this interpretation by tracing and demystifying its origins. This phrase is from her "The Balkans: From Discovery to Invention," *Slavic Review* 53/2 (1994): 460.

4. One of the most celebrated examples of this argument is George Kennan, "The Balkan Crisis: 1913 and 1993," *The New York Review of Books* 40/13, July 15, 1993.

5. "Serbia: Relief in Europe as Voters Hand Tadic Narrow Second-Round Win," *Radio Free Europe/Radio Liberty*, February 4, 2008. For the international

community, the police reform deal in Bosnia becomes "A Breakthrough on the Road to Europe," *Office for the High Representative Press Release*, April 16, 2008.

6. The figures in this section and the quotes are from Jerry Z. Muller, "Us and Them: The Enduring Power of Ethnic Nationalism," *Foreign Affairs* 87 (March/April 2008).

7. Ernest Gellner, "Nationalism," *Theory and Society* 10/6 (November 1981).

8. Charles Tilly, "War-Making and State-Making as Organized Crime," in *Bringing the State Back In*, Peter B. Evans, Dietrich Reuschemeyer, and Theda Skocpol (eds) (Cambridge: Cambridge University Press, 1985).

9. The figures on heroin trafficking are from the German Federal Criminal Police Office and the Swiss police. They are quoted by *Time Magazine* Balkan correspondent Dejan Anastasijevic in "Organized Crime in the Western Balkans," *HUMSEC Working Papers* 1 (2006), retrievable at http://www.humsec.eu. The figure on Balkan immigration in the 1990s results from accumulated 2002 Eurostat estimates (New Cronos) as presented by Corrado Bonifazi, Cinzia Conti, and Marija Mamolo, "Balkan International Migration in the 1990s" *Demobalk* 8 (2006).

10. On the Transparency International ranking, see the latest *Corruption Perception Index*, http://www.transparency.org. The Greek and Macedonian crime rates (973 per 100,000 inhabitants for the former and 977 per 100,000 for the latter) are from the year 2000 and can be found at *The Eighth United Nations Survey on Crime Trends and the Operations of Criminal Justice Systems*, http://www.unodc.org.

11. Andrew Cockburn, "21st Century Slaves," *National Geographic* 204/3 (September 2003). Roberto Saviano, *Gomorrah: A Personal Journey into the Violent International Empire of Naples' Organized Crime System* (New York: Farrar, Straus and Giroux, 2007).

12. The most comprehensive and updated work on nation-building, including Europe's role in it, is arguably that of James Dobbins from the RAND corporation. See James Dobbins et al., *Europe's Role in Nation-Building: From the Balkans to the Congo* (Santa Monica: RAND Corporation, 2008).

13. I borrow the term from Gerald Knaus and Markus Cox, "Building Democracy After Conflict: The 'Helsinki Moment' in Southeastern Europe," *Journal of Democracy* 16/1 (January 2005). Knaus and Cox use "member state–building" mostly to describe the process that leads countries to EU membership, in contrast with what they call "authoritarian state–building," as seen in Bosnia and Kosovo. I seek to encompass both approaches by using "member state–building" in a more gradualist fashion.

14. According to Elisabeth Pond, the total bilateral and multilateral European assistance to the Balkans amounted to some €33 billion ($44 billion) between 2001 and 2005 only. See her *Endgame in the Balkans: Regime Change, European Style* (Washington, D.C.: Brookings Institution, 2006), 278. EU assistance totalled €4.65 billion ($6.17 billion) between 2000 and 2006. The comparison between the per capita assistance to Bosnia and Germany

in 2000 USD is in James Dobbins et al., *America's Role in Nation-Building: From Germany to Iraq* (Santa Monica: RAND, 2003), 237. The comparison between Kosovo and Afghanistan is made by the International Commission on the Balkans, *The Balkans in Europe's Future* (2005), 7–8. http://www.balkan-commission.org.

15. Karen Smith, *European Union Foreign Policy in a Changing World* (Cambridge: Polity, 2003), 79ff.

16. For a similar argument, Judy Batt, "The Stabilization/Integration Dilemma," in *The Western Balkans: Moving On*, ed. Judy Batt, Chaillot paper 70, Paris, EU Institute for Security Studies, October 2004.

17. I am grateful to Ed Joseph at Johns Hopkins' SAIS for discussing this argument with me. His position on this question is well explained in Edward P. Joseph, "Ownership Is Over-rated," *SAIS Review* 27/2 (Summer–Fall 2007). The most eloquent example of the opposite line of reasoning is Gerald Knaus and Felix Martin, "Travails of the European Raj," *Journal of Democracy* 14/3 (July 2003). For an illustrative comparison of the two positions, "Debate: Does the International Presence in the Balkans Require Radical Restructuring? Gerald Knaus vs. Nicholas Whyte," *NATO Review*, Winter 2004.

18. The regular reporting by the International Crisis Group on these issues is essential for appreciating the details. On the cases discussed here, see "Breaking the Kosovo Stalemate: Europe's Responsibility," *Europe Report* 185, August 21, 2007; "Ensuring Bosnia's Future: A New International Engagement Strategy," *Europe Report* 180, February 15, 2007; "Macedonia: Wobbling toward Europe," *Europe Briefing* 41, January 12, 2006; "Montenegro's Referendum," *Europe Briefing* 42, May 30, 2006.

19. Ceric made the point to explain how the liberal and tolerant variant of European Islam is deeply intertwined with the principle of the equality of all men before the law. Reis-L-Ulama Dr. Mustafa Ceric, Gran Mufti of Bosnia, "A Declaration of European Muslims," *Radio Free Europe/Radio Liberty*, March 16, 2006. http://www.rferl.org.

20. Were it not for a quarrel with Greece over the official name of Macedonia (which is also a Greek region), Skopje would already be negotiating the terms of its NATO membership. Albania and Croatia joined the Alliance in April 2009.

21. A recent occasion for this attitude has been provided by Kosovo's independence. Louis Amado, the Foreign Minister of Portugal presiding over the EU at the time, declared that Kosovo was "key to the credibility of Europe's foreign policy", *BBC News*, "EU Ministers Vow Unity on Kosovo," September 8, 2007. For the European Commission, the Kosovo issue was the "litmus test of an immediate nature in order to retain [the EU's] credibility" (http://ec.europa.eu).

22. International Commission on the Balkans, *The Balkans in Europe's Future* ..., 6.

23. These are among the measures outlined in European Commission, "Western Balkans: Enhancing the European Perspective," Brussels, March 3, 2008.

Chapter 3: Turkish Ironies

1. The TGV is France's high-speed rail service. The quotes are from three speeches by Commissioner Olli Rehn: the first in Prague on September 18, 2008; the second in Brussels on November 6, 2006; the third in Strasbourg on March 15, 2006. http://ec.europa.eu.

2. Web site of the General Staff, Turkish Armed Forces, April 27, 2007. Translation by the *Turkish Daily News*. http://www.turkishdailynews.com.

3. For an overview of the genesis of modern Turkey, see Ahmad Feroz, *The Making of Modern Turkey* (London: Routledge, 1993).

4. Quoted in Christopher de Bellaigue: "Turkey at the Turning Point?" The *New York Review of Books*, Vol. 54, Number 16, October 25, 2007.

5. Revealingly, "No Islamic law, but no coup either!" was the slogan chanted by the masses crowding the streets of Ankara and Istanbul in that hot spring of 2007 that preceded Gül's election.

6. European Stability Initiative, *Islamic Calvinists: Change and Conservatism in Central Anatolia*, September 19, 2005. The report refers in particular to the town of Kayseri, a showcase of innovation and entrepreneurship.

7. Nathalie Tocci, "Unpacking European Discourses: Conditionality, Impact and Prejudice in EU-Turkey Relations," *Quaderni IAI* (Rome: Istituto Affari Internazionali, 2007), 8.

8. *EU-Turkey Negotiating Framework* 2005, 6. http://www.dtm.gov.tr.

9. Kemal Dervis et al., "Turkey and the EU Budget: Prospects and Issues," *CEPS EU-Turkey Working Papers* 6 (August 2004).

10. International Crisis Group, "Turkey and Europe: the Way Ahead," *Europe Report* 184, August 17, 2007.

11. The notion of "privileged partnership" is particularly strong in the conservative circles of Austria, Germany, and France. See Matthias Wissmann, "Eine 'Privilegierte Partnerschaft' als Alternative zu Einer EU-Vollmitgliedschaft der Türkei," Konrad Adenauer Stiftung, January 22, 2004. Karl-Theodor Zu Guttenberg, "Die Beziehungen zwischen der Türkei und der EU—eine Privilegierte Partnerschaft," *Aktuelle Papier* 33 (2004). I thank Martina Warning for her research assistance in reviewing the German debate on this issue.

12. "French in Armenia 'Genocide' Row," *BBC News*, October 12, 2006.

13. According to a Financial Times/Harris poll of June 18, 2007, Italian and British support for the Turkish EU bid stands at 31 and 23 percent, respectively. http://www.harrisinteractive.com.

14. An unnamed Turkish stakeholder, quoted in "The EU and Turkey: Drifting Apart?" Key Conclusions of the 4th Bosphorus Conference, Istanbul October 5–6, 2007, 2. http://www.cer.org.uk.

15. The Turkish authorities have long been engaged in a bloody confrontation with the extremists of the Kurdistan Workers Party (also known by its acronym, PKK), which may have caused up to 35,000 casualties.

16. Here I follow John Roberts, "The Turkish Gate: Energy Transit and Security Issues," *Turkish Policy Quarterly* 3/4 (Winter 2004).

17. Barry Buzan and Ole Wæver, *Regions and Powers: The Structure of International Security* (Cambridge: Cambridge University Press, 2002), 377–395.

18. Fiona Hill and Ömer Taşpınar, "Turkey and Russia: Axis of the Excluded?" *Survival* 48 (Spring 2006). Dietrich Jung, "Turkey's Future: EU Member or 'Islamist Rogue State'?" (Copenhagen: Danish Institute for International Studies, January 2007).

Chapter 4: The Remains of the Wall

1. For the quotes in this section and an account of this event, "Poland and Ukraine host Euro 2012" *BBC News*, April 18, 2007 at http://news.bbc.co.uk.

2. Franklin Foer, *How Soccer Explains the World: An Unlikely Theory of Globalization* (New York: HarperCollins, 2004).

3. See, for instance, John S. Dryzek and Leslie Templeman Holmes, *Post-Communist Democratization: Political Discourses across Thirteen Countries* (Cambridge: Cambridge University Press, 2002), or the seminal Juan J. Linz and Alfred Stefan, *Problems of Democratic Transition and Consolidation: Southern Europe, South America, and Post-Communist Europe* (Baltimore: John Hopkins University Press, 1996).

4. These are the nominal GDP figures from International Monetary Fund (IMF), *World Economic Outlook Database,* October 2007. The figures for the economic "miracle" of authoritarian Belarus are more debatable. Nevertheless, the IMF puts its nominal GDP per capita at $4,013.

5. On drug smuggling to Europe, United Nations Office on Drugs and Crime, *The Opium Economy in Afghanistan: An International Problem* (New York: United Nations, 2003) and "Russia Must Stop Flood of Afghan Heroin," *Reuters*, October 5, 2007. For the figures on emigration from Moldova and Ukraine, Michael Jandl, *Moldova Seeks Stability Amid Mass Emigration* (Washington, D.C.: Migration Information Source, Migration Policy Institute, December 2003); Olena Malynovska, *Caught Between East and West, Ukraine Struggles with Its Migration Policy* (Washington, D.C.: Migration Information Source, Migration Policy Institute, January 2006). On the Belarus arms trade, Mark Harrington, "Iran set to acquire S-300PTs from Belarus," *Jane's Defence Systems News*, January 17, 2008.

6. Andrew Wilson, *Virtual Politics: Faking Democracy in the Post-Soviet World* (New Haven: Yale University Press, 2005).

7. World Bank, *Worldwide Governance Indicators* (2007), accessible at http://www.worldbank.org.

8. On the link between democratization and conflict potential, Jack Snyder and Edward Mansfield, "Democratization and the Danger of War," *International Security* 20/1 (Summer 1995).

9. Fareed Zakaria. *The Future of Freedom: Illiberal Democracy at Home and Abroad* (New York: W.W. Norton & Company, 2004).

10. Adam Przeworski and Fernando Limongi "Modernization: Theories and Facts" *World Politics* 49/2 (January 1997).

11. These three phrases are extracted from the EU Neighborhood Policy's *Action Plans* between the EU and Moldova, Georgia, and Ukraine, respectively. http://ec.europa.eu.

12. The figure for Central Europe is calculated on the basis of the allocation of the main EU assistance instruments (PHARE for institution building and economic and social cohesion; ISPA for transport and environmental projects; SAPHARD for agriculture) to the 10 Central European states that accessed the EU in 2004 and 2007. The figure for Eastern Europe is provided by the European Commission in the *ENP Country Reports* for each of the six former Soviet states. http://ec.europa.eu.

13. Partnership and Cooperation Agreements between the EU and the former Soviet republics contain a "suspension clause" to freeze the agreement if countries move away from their commitments. It has never been activated.

14. These statements are, respectively, by then EU Commission's President Romano Prodi (in "De vraag is: waar houdt Europa op?" *De Volkskrant*, November 27, 2002) and Commissioner Gunther Verheugen (in "The EU's Unwanted Stranger?" *EurActive*, July 18, 2002).

15. Robert L. Larsson, *Russia's Energy Policy: Security Dimensions and Russia's Reliability as an Energy Supplier* (Stockholm: Swedish Defence Research Agency, March 2006), 4.

16. See, for example, in relation to Ukraine, Mikhail Molchanov, "Ukraine and the European Union: a Perennial Neighbour?" *Journal of European Integration* 26 (December 2004): 460.

17. As Virgil explains in the *Aeneid*: "Two gates of steel (the name of Mars they bear,/ And still are worship'd with religious fear)/ Before his temple stand: the dire abode,/ And the fear'd issues of the furious god,/ Are fenc'd with brazen bolts; without the gates,/ The wary guardian Janus doubly waits." Virgil, *The Aeneid*, Book VII, trans. John Dryden, ed. Stephen G. Thomas (eBooks@Adelaide, 2004).

18. For these figures, see Inna Pidluska, "Justice and Home Affairs Beyond Enlargement. What Kind of Border?" in *The EU and Ukraine: Neighbours, Friends, Partners?* ed. Ann Lewis (London: Federal Trust, 2001), 243.

19. European Commission, "A Strong European Neighbourhood Policy," Brussels, December 5, 2007, 6.

20. On "Window to Europe," Ahto Lobjankas, "Belarus: EU-Funded Broadcasts Set to Begin," *Radio Free Europe/Radio Liberty*, May 24, 2006.

21. This is the scene described by Ukrainian journalist Tatiana Silina in "Want an EU Visa? Then Sing . . . ," *EU Observer*, May 23, 2007.

22. Thanks to Nicu Popescu for pointing this out to me.

23. European Commission, "ENPI Interregional Programme, Strategy Paper 2007–2013, and Indicative Programme 2007–2010," 16.

24. In the midst of the financial crisis, a similar appeal was put forward by the leading Eastern Europe an economist Anders Aaslund, "The Case

for Ukraine," Realtime Economic Issues Watch (Washington, DC: Peterson Institute for International Economics, February 26, 2009). http://www. petersoninstitute.org.

Chapter 5: Russia's Roller Coaster

1. For a detailed account of these events, an analysis of Gorchakov's foreign policy and its impact on contemporary Russia, Flemming Splidsboel Hansen, "Past and Future Meet: Aleksandr Gorchakov and Russian Foreign Policy," *Europe-Asia Studies* 54/3 (May 2002).

2. For the data cited here and an overview of the Russian economy in the early 1990s, see William Cooper, "The Economy," in *Russia: A Country Study*, ed. Glenn E. Curtis (Washington, DC: GPO for the Library of Congress, A996).

3. For a detailed account of the Yeltsin years, see Lilia Shevtsova, *Yeltsin's Russia: Myths and Reality* (Washington, DC: Brookings Institution, 1998).

4. Based upon the study of the biographies of 1,016 leading figures in the Putin administration, Olga Kryshtanovskaya of the Moscow-based Center for the Study of Elites has come to the conclusion that up to 78 percent of them might have a background in the Russian intelligence service. Peter Finn, "In Russia, a Secretive Force Widens," *Washington Post*, December 12, 2006.

5. Robert Coalson, "The End of the Russian Federation?" *Radio Free Europe/Radio Liberty*, September 23, 2004.

6. "Russia Rejects Powell Criticism," *BBC News*, September 15, 2004. http://news.bbc.co.uk.

7. Michael McFaul and Kathryn Stoner-Weiss, "The Myth of the Authoritarian Model: How Putin's Crackdown Holds Russia Back," *Foreign Affairs* 87 (January/February 2008), 74. The murder rate is also from this article (p. 75). For the data on alcoholism in Russia, see "40,000 Annually Die in Russia of Alcoholism," *Kommersant*, September 18, 2007. The figures on HIV/AIDS are provided by the Joint United Nations Programme on HIV/AIDS. http://www.pepfar.gov.

8. Thomas Graham, "A World Without Russia?" Paper presented at a Jamestown Foundation Conference, Washington, D.C., June 9, 1999, Carnegie Endowment for International Peace. http://www.carnegieendowment. org.

9. An excellent account of these different dynamics is in Dmitry Trenin, *The End of Eurasia: Russia on the Border between Geopolitics and Globalization* (Washington, D.C.: Carnegie Endowment for International Peace, 2001).

10. The contemporary roller coaster traces back to ice slides built around St. Petersburg since the 15th century. In several European languages, including French, Italian, and Spanish, roller coaster still translates as "Russian mountains." The Russian term for it literally translates as "American mountains."

11. These quotes are from Iver B. Neumann, "Russia as Europe's Other" *EUI-RSCAS Working Papers* 34 (Fiesole: European University Institute, Robert Schuman Centre of Advanced Studies, 1996), 33, 23, and 6.

12. The most extensive and prescient exposé on EU-Russia relations is arguably Michael Emerson, *The Elephant and the Bear: The European Union, Russia, and their Near Abroads* (Brussels: CEPS, 2001).

13. In recent years, Italian energy company ENI has sealed several deals with Gazprom. German Ruhrgas owns about 6 percent of the Gazprom shares. French GDF and Total have longstanding partnerships with Russia, including the development of a number of Russian gas fields.

14. The poll "Voices from Russia: Society, Democracy, Europe" was conducted jointly by the Levada Centre and the EU-Russia Centre in February 2007.

15. Quoted in Neil S. MacFarlane, "Russia, the West and European Security," in *Survival* 35/3 (1993): 9.

16. Mikhail Gorbachev and Alexander Lebedev, "Arrogance Exposes the Cracks in Europe's Expanding Empire," *Financial Times*, July 26, 2005.

17. An interesting analysis of Moscow's justification of the war, can be found in Quentin Peel, "Russia's Reversal: Where Next for Humanitarian Intervention?" *Financial Times*, August 22, 2008.

18. Council of the European Union, "Extraordinary European Council: Presidency Conclusions" Brussels, September 1, 2008, 2. "Bush: Russian Response to Georgia 'Disproportional' " *Reuters*, August 10, 2008.

19. Nicolas Sarkozy: "La Russie Doit Se Retirer Sans Délai de Géorgie," *Le Figaro*, August 17, 2008. http://www.lefigaro.fr.

20. Ivan Krastev: "Russia and the Georgia War: The Great-Power Trap" *opendemocracy*, August 19, 2008. http://www.opendemocracy.net.

21. This sentence by the great novelist was quoted by none other than Vladimir Putin in a commentary he wrote commemorating the 50th anniversary of the EU. Vladimir Putin, "50 Years of the European Integration and Russia," published in European media on March 25, 2007. http://www.kremlin.ru.

Chapter 6: A Sea of Troubles

1. The Mediterranean, which etymologically means, "in the midst of lands," was tellingly referred to by Arabs as "Bahr Al Rum" ("Sea of the Romans"). This Moroccan tale is recounted by Mohamed Berrada and Abdelmajid Kaddouri, *La Méditerranée Marocaine* (Paris: Maisonneuve & Larose, 2000), 24.

2. Report by the High-Level Advisory Group established at the initiative of the President of the European Commission, *Dialogue Between Peoples and Cultures in the Euro-Mediterranean Area* (Brussels: October 2003), 4. Fernand Braudel's quote is from his seminal *The Mediterranean and the Mediterranean World in the Age of Philip II*, I. trans. Siân Reynolds, 2nd ed. (London: Fontana, 1966), 761.

3. In 2008, an estimated 67,000 migrants arrived in Europe by sea ("Trouble with Figures," *The Economist*, January 31, 2009). That is less than 3% of all the migrants reaching Europe that year.

4. The figures on France are from Vikki Valentine, "Economic Despair, Racism Drive French Riots," *National Public Radio*, November 8, 2005, http://www.npr.org. The figures on education in Denmark are from the OECD and cited in the outlook on Muslims in Denmark published by the EU-sponsored Web site http://www.euro-islam.info. For the population projection of European Muslims, "Look out Europe, They Say," *The Economist*, June 22, 2006. The latter article also offers a rather unforgiving parallel between European Muslims and the wealthier and more integrated Muslim population in the United States.

5. The population projection and illiteracy rates are from the United Nations Development Programme, Arab Fund for Economic and Social Development, *Arab Human Development Report* (New York, 2002), 37 and 25, respectively. The data on economic growth and unemployment are from the World Bank's World Development Indicators, in "Middle East and North Africa: Regional Data from the WDI Database," http://www.worldbank.org. The figure on remittances is from 2005 and is quoted in Catherine Wihtol de Wenden, "Europe: Immigration Unwanted," *European Affairs* 7 (Fall/Winter 2006).

6. Pew Global Attitudes Project, *Muslims in Europe: Economic Worries Top Concerns About Religious and Cultural Identity* (Washington, DC July 2006), 3.

7. See Olivier Roy, "EuroIslam: The Jihad Within?" *The National Interest* 71 (Spring 2003).

8. Pew Global Attitudes Project, *Muslims in Europe . . .* 11 and 7.

9. Runnymede Trust: Commission on British Muslims and Islamophobia, *Islamophobia: A Challenge for Us All* (London: Runnymede Trust, 1997).

10. For an optimistic view on this, see Amel Boubekeur and Samir Amghar, "Islamist Parties in the Maghreb and Their Links with EU: Mutual Influences and the Dynamics of Democratisation," *Euromesco Papers* 55 (October 2006). For a more skeptical take: Nathan J. Brown, Amr Hamzawy, and Marina Ottaway, "Islamist Movements and the Democratic Process in the Arab World," *Carnegie Papers Middle East Series* 67 (March 2006).

11. The baskets have now become the "dimensions" of the Organization for Security and Cooperation in Europe. For a parallel between the Mediterranean and CSCE processes, see Sharon Pardo and Lior Zemer, "The Institutional Challenge of the Euro-Mediterranean Neighbourhood Space," The Centre for the Study of European Politics and Society, Ben-Gurion University of the Negev.

12. This breaks down as the 27 EU Member States, plus Morocco, Algeria, Tunisia, Egypt, the Palestinian Authority, Israel, Syria, Jordan, Lebanon, and Turkey. Mauritania and Albania joined in 2007. At the time of this writing, Libya—an observer of the Barcelona Process since 1999—is yet to become a full member.

13. For a trenchant critique of this sequencing, see William Easterly, "The Ideology of Development," *Foreign Policy*, July/August 2007. For a more

positive assessment, in the case of the EU's Mediterranean policies, see Daniel Muller Jentsch, *Deeper Integration and Trade in Services in the Euro-Mediterranean Region—Southern Dimensions of the European Neighbourhood Policy* (Washington, D.C.: World Bank, 2004).

14. Alvaro de Soto, UN Special Representative for the Middle East Peace Process, *End of Mission Report* (May 2007), 31, 9, and 26.

15. Eneko Landaburu, EU Commission's Director General in charge of the European Neighbourhood Policy (speaking at a conference at the Palais D'Egmont, Brussels, 23 January 2006).

16. Nicolas Sarkozy, "Discours du Président de la République sur le thème de l'Union de la Méditerranée," Tangier, October 23, 2007. http://www.elysee.fr.

17. The Arab-Maghreb Union consists of Algeria, Morocco, Mauritania, Tunisia, and Libya. The rivalry between Algeria and Morocco over the Western Sahara has greatly accounted for the stagnation of this arrangement. The Agadir agreement aims to bring together the like-minded economies of Morocco, Tunisia, Egypt, and Jordan.

18. "Open Letter to Tony Blair from the Ten Ministers of Foreign Affairs of the Mediterranean Member States of the European Union," *Le Monde*, July 10, 2007, English version at http://commentisfree.guardian.co.uk.

19. In 1931, Pope Pius XI thus described subsidiarity, "Just as it is gravely wrong to take from individuals what they can accomplish by their own initiative and industry and give it to the community, so also it is an injustice and at the same time a grave evil and disturbance of right order to assign to a greater and higher association what lesser and subordinate organizations can do" (*Encyclical Quadrigesimo Anno*, Vatican City, 1931. http://www.vatican.va).

20. Hugo Grotius, *The Freedom of the Seas, or, the right which belongs to the Dutch to take Part in the East Indian Trade: a Dissertation*, trans. Ralph van Deman Magoffin with a revision of the Latin text (1633; New York: Oxford University Press, 1916). Jacques Attali, an advisor to President Sarkozy, evoked a similar parallel to maritime freedom when presenting his views on the Union for the Mediterranean. To that, however, he also added that the Mediterranean is a time bomb. See "La Méditerranée est une bombe à retardement," *EurActiv.fr*, March 31, 2008. http://www.euractiv.fr.

Chapter 7: The Wide West

1. Once again, the most persuasive interpretation of this argument is Kagan's *Of Paradise and Power*.

2. This is what political scientist Karl W. Deutsch called "security community" in his seminal *Political Community and the North Atlantic Area* (Princeton, NJ: Princeton University Press, 1957).

3. Timothy Garton Ash, *Free World: Why a Crisis of the West Reveals the Opportunity of Our Time* (London: Penguin, 2004).

4. This phrase has been used by senior members of all of the U.S. administrations since the end of the Cold War. The strongest statement arguably remains that of President George H. Bush, "A Europe Whole and Free," in Mainz (West Germany) on May 31, 1989, retrievable at http://usa.usembassy.de.

5. Here I follow Charles A. Kupchan, *The End of the American Era: US Foreign Policy and the Geopolitics of the Twenty-first Century* (New York: Vintage Books, 2002), 132.

6. The EU's criteria were spelled out in European Council, "Conclusions of the Presidency" (Copenhagen, June 21–22, 1993), 13, retrievable at http://ue.eu.int. For the United States, see White House, *The National Security Strategy of the United States of America* (Washington, D.C., 2006). Although with less prominence, the promotion of democracy and human rights similarly featured among the three main priorities of the 2000 National Security Strategy of the Clinton administration.

7. The figures for the EU are retrieved from EC Regulation 1886/2006 of December 20, 2006. The U.S. data refer to the fiscal year 2004 and can be found in USAID, *Democracy Rising* (Washington, D.C., 2005), 25.

8. The literature on democracy promotion is very extensive. For a comprehensive overview, see, for instance, Thomas Carothers, *Aiding Democracy Abroad: the Learning Curve* (Washington, D.C.: Carnegie Endowment for International Peace, 1999). An in-depth survey of some European variants on the issue is Richard Youngs, ed., *Survey of European Democracy Promotion Policies 2000–2006* (Madrid: FRIDE, 2007).

9. For a similar interpretation, Jeffrey Kopstein, "The Transatlantic Divide over Democracy Promotion," *The Washington Quarterly* (Spring 2006): 86–87.

10. Retrieved from the USAID Web site at: http://www.usaid.gov.

11. Richard Youngs, *Trans-Atlantic Cooperation on Middle East Reform: a European Misjudgment?* (London: Foreign Policy Centre, December 2004), 11.

12. Tamara Cofman Wittes, "Promoting Democracy in the Arab World: The Challenge of Joint Action," *The International Spectator* 39/4 (2004).

13. A comprehensive study on this case is Bruce Jentleson and Christopher Whytock, "Who 'Won' Libya? The Force-Diplomacy Debate and Its Implications for Theory and Policy," *International Security* 30 (Winter 2005/06), 47–86.

14. Cyprus is not a NATO member and Turkey has blocked its participation in joint EU–NATO meetings. Correspondingly, Cyprus is one of the staunchest opponents of Turkey's EU membership.

15. In the European neighborhood, operations under the European Security and Defence Policy have been active in Moldova, Georgia, the Palestinian Territories, and throughout the Balkans. This growing presence has led some scholars to call for a revision of the existing arrangements between the EU and NATO, and to call for a "right of first choice" of the EU *vis-à-vis* NATO in the European neighborhood. Roberto Menotti and Paolo Brandimarte, "It's Time to Clarify the 'Constructive Ambiguity' in the NATO–EU Security Relationship," *Europe's World* (Spring 2007).

16. U.S. Senator Richard Lugar is among those who advocate the NATO protection in case of a cutoff of energy supplies to an allied country. Vladimir Socor, "Lugar Urges Active Role for NATO in Energy Security Policy," *Eurasia Daily Monitor* 3 (222) (December 2006).

17. For example, half of all EU neighbors, including all North African and Middle Eastern countries, belong to the so-called G-77 group of developing countries, which, together with China, has presented a common negotiating bloc on the replacement of the Kyoto protocol. On transatlantic collaboration in the fields of energy and environment, see *2007 EU–US Summit Statement: Energy Security, Efficiency, and Climate Change*, Washington, D.C., http://www.eu2007.de.

Conclusion: A Sensible Europe

1. The most controversial instance here is the 2006 lecture in which the Pope famously quoted a 14-century Byzantine emperor saying, "Show me just what Muhammad brought that was new and there you will find things only evil and inhuman, such as his command to spread by the sword the faith he preached." The lecture was followed by an apology of the Vatican and by an "Open Letter to His Holiness Pope Benedict the XVI," signed by 38 Muslim intellectuals on October 12, 2006.

2. His Holiness Benedict the XVI, *Address at the Basilica of St. John Lateran*, Rome, June 6, 2005. See also Joseph Ratzinger and Marcello Pera, *Without Roots: Europe, Relativism, Christianity, Islam* (New York: Basic Books, 2006).

3. Quoted by Timothy Garton Ash in the Adam von Trott Memorial Lecture "Are there Moral Foundations of European Power?" Oxford, November 30, 2004, 19, http://www.sant.ox.ac.uk.

4. I owe this simile to veteran Finnish scholar Pertti Joenniemi.

5. A similar argument is made by Nick Witney, the former head of the European Defence Agency, in "Re-energising Europe's Security and Defence Policy,"*Policy Paper*, London, European Council on Foreign Relations (July 2008): 14–28.

6. I received this information from Benita Ferrero-Waldner, the EU Commissioner for External Relations, in a meeting at the EU Committee of the Regions in Brussels on September 19, 2007. An account of this and other Russian initiatives on cross-border cooperation with Europe is in Galina Stolyarova, "Economic Experiments at the Border," *St. Petersburg Times*, June 26, 2007.

7. Francis Fukuyama, "Russia and a New Democratic Realism," *Financial Times*, September 3, 2008. The term "democratic realism," Fukuyama acknowledges elsewhere, was originally coined by neo-conservative commentator Charles Krauthammer. Here, the attribute "new" would appear to signal precisely the need to distance U.S. policy from the controversial meaning that the democracy promotion came to acquire during the Bush administration.

8. Andrew Moravcsik has gone so far as to argue that Europe's legitimacy stems from its transparency and accountability rather than from its democratic credentials (see his ''In Defense of the 'Democratic Deficit': Reassessing the Legitimacy of the European Union,'' *Journal of Common Market Studies* 40/4 (2002).

9. Richard Youngs, ''Is European Democracy Promotion on the Wane?'' *CEPS Working Document* 292, May 2008, 11.

10. This is what Thomas Carothers from the Carnegie Endowment refers to as the ''sequencing fallacy'' (see his ''How Democracies Emerge: The 'Sequencing' Fallacy,'' *Journal of Democracy* 18/1 (January 2007).

11. The phrase is attributed to Nicolas Sarkozy by Charlemagne, ''A Worrying New World Order,'' *The Economist*, September 13, 2008. See also National Intelligence Council, *Global Trends 2025: A Transformed World*, Washington, D.C., November 2008. http://www.dni.gov.

12. ''Non-polar,'' ''post-American,'' and ''neo-polar'' world are some of the recent definitions. See Richard N. Haass, ''The Age of Nonpolarity: What Will Follow U.S. Dominance,'' *Foreign Affairs* 87 (May/June 2008). Fareed Zakaria, *The Post-American World* (New York: W.W. Norton & Company, 2008).

13. Niall Ferguson, ''A World Without Power,'' *Foreign Policy* (July/August 2004).

14. See Charlemagne, ''Brussels Rules OK'' *The Economist*, September 20, 2007.

15. This is the argument, for example, put forward by Jeremy Rifkin, *The European Dream* . . . , 358–364.

Index

Abkhazia, 56, 61, 75
Afghanistan, 31, 32, 55, 99
African Union, 114
Agadir agreement, 88
Albania, 1, 28, 30, 33, 35, 38, 81, 91, 126, 132
Alexander of Macedon (the Great), 79
Algeria, 1, 2, 23, 85, 132, 133; "Algerian syndrome," 97
Al Qaeda, 113
Alighieri, Dante, 112, 113
Anatolian peninsula, 51
appeasement, 72
Arab Human Development Report, 81
Arab-Israeli conflict and EU policy, 85–86
Arab-Maghreb Union, 88
Armenia, 23, 54, 56, 63; "genocide" issue, 48, 51
Association of Southeast Asian Nations (ASEAN), 114
Atatürk. *See* Kemal, Mustafa
Austria, 11, 47, 76, 110, 127
autocracy, 2, 25, 56, 63, 79, 83, 111
Azerbaijan, 2, 54, 55, 56, 63

Baker, James, 38
balance of power 4, 74, 75

Balkans, 1, 2, 5, 7, 22, 27–40, 50, 55, 94, 100, 104, 105, 106, 111, 115; accession deadline, 39; barbarity, 28–31; constitutions, Europe's involvement, 32–33; Contact Group, 108; corruption in, 31, 39; member state-building in, 32; multi-ethnic arrangements in, 32–33, 35; organized crime in, 30; ownership, 34–36; stabilization and association process, 33–34
Baltic Sea, 76, 108
Baltic States, 71, 73
banlieues, 81
Barcelona Process, 84, 87, 88, 90
Belarus, 2, 11, 23, 54, 58, 63, 64, 98, 128
Belgium, 29
Benelux, 108
Berlin Wall, 13, 84, 93
Bertelsmann Transformation Index, 2
Beslan (school siege), 69
Bill and Melinda Gates Foundation, 113
Black Sea, 51, 61, 100, 108; Fleet, 58
Blair, Tony, 88
"blue card" program, 106
Bonaparte, Napoleon, 3

Bosnia and Herzegovina, 28, 29, 30, 31, 32, 33, 34, 35, 36, 37, 38, 81, 105, 125; High Representative in, 27, 34, 36; ownership in, 36; police force, 27, 29
Braudel, Fernand, 79
Brazil, 113
Britain. *See* United Kingdom
Bulgaria, 18, 31, 39, 71, 76
Bush, George H., 134
Bush, George W., 91, 92, 97, 110
Büyükanit, Yasar, 43

Camus, Albert, 16
Canary Islands, 80
Cardiff City Hall, 53
Casablanca, 83
Caspian Sea, 60
Catherine the Great, 17
Caucasus, 2, 22, 51, 55, 64, 74, 77, 115
Central Asia, 70, 74, 76; as energy Eldorado, 51
Central Europe, 29, 32, 33, 45, 70, 76, 93, 98, 100; EU enlargement toward, 4, 18, 19, 50, 58, 59, 68, 99, 105; financial assistance to, 57–58, 84, 129; financial crisis in, 21, 64; governance standards in, 55; missile defense system in, 73; perceptions of Russia in, 71, 77
Ceric, Mustafa, 38
Ceuta, 80
Charter for Peace and Stability, 85
Chechnya, 68, 72
China, 7, 11, 35, 70, 74, 113
Chirac, Jacques, 92
Christendom, 113
Churchill, Winston, 22, 70
civil society, 18, 90, 96, 112
Clinton, Bill, 91, 134
Cold War, 13, 63, 77, 87, 95–96, 99, 109
Colored Revolutions, 55, 64
Conference for Security and Cooperation in Europe, 84
Conventional Forces in Europe Treaty, 73

COPPS (EU Police Coordinating Office for Palestinian Police Support), 86
corruption, 18, 24, 31, 39, 55, 56, 72
Coudenhove-Kalergi, Count Richard, 104
Council of Europe, 22, 51
Crimea, 58; Crimean War, 67
Croatia, 5, 28, 31, 33, 36, 37, 48, 53, 126
crusades, 3
Cyprus, 2, 18, 49; and Turkey, conflict between, 99, 134
Czech Republic, 18, 71, 73, 86, 99, 108

Dayton accords, 33
De Gaulle, Charles, 22
Delphi (oracle), 22
Del Ponte, Carla, 36–37
democracy, 2, 8, 11, 13, 18, 23, 36, 47, 56, 57, 68, 76, 99, 104; and autocracy, 63; promotion of, 95–97; transition to, 18, 54, 58, 93, 110–12, 115
Denmark, 73, 81
Derrida, Jacques, 10, 14
de Soto, Alvaro, 86
D'Estaing, Valery Giscard, 47
dictatorship, 4, 11, 14, 17, "of the law," 68, "of relativism," 103
Diyarbakir, 50
Dostoevsky, Fyodor, 76, 78

Eastern Europe, 1, 17, 53–65, 100, 106, 111; EU financial assistance to, 57; frozen conflicts, 56, 61; poverty in, 55
Eastern Partnership, 63
Economist, The, 3
Eden, Garden of, 54
effective multilateralism, 14
Egypt, 23, 86, 98, 111, 132, 133
elections, 42, 43, 49, 57; and democratic transition, 54–55, 96, 97
energy, 1, 2, 3, 52, 60, 70, 71, 76, 77, 88, 100, 101, 110, 114;, dependence, 1, 76; disruptions of supplies, 59; reform and, 60–61

Energy Charter Treaty, 76
Engels, Friedrich, 70
Erdogan, Recep Tayyip, 43
Erzurum, 50
Estonia, 18, 58, 109
ethno-nationalist conflicts, 25
Eurabia, 81
Euroatlantic integration, 63, 94, 99, 100
Euro-Mediterranean Partnership. *See* Barcelona process
Europe, anti-Americanism in, 10; anti-Turkish sentiments in, 47, 48, 49; Concert of, 67; democracy in, 8, 11, 13, 16, 95; demographic predicament of, 21; "difference" of, 15–17, 19, 103, 109–10; economic recovery in, 11; ethnic "disaggregation" in, 29; European project, 3–4, 12, 21; foreign direct investment in, 13; "Fortress," 6; *Grande Europe*, 71; identity, 3, 7, 103, 104; identity crisis in, 8, 22, 48, 51, 64, 104; imperial metaphor, 16–17; inter-state integration in, 12; Islam and, 3, 83; Islamo-phobia in, 82–83; labor market in 1, 20, 21, 41; modernity of, 44–45; multiculturalism in, 7, 20, 48, 80; Muslim minorities in, 80–83; "new" and "old," 10; peace in, 1, 4–7, 11, 12, 14, 80, 115; post-war integration project of, 9; power constellation in, 7, 8, 77, 93, 103; "privatization of faith," 14; rule of law in, 14; social market economy in, 13, 14
European Coal and Steel Community, 12
European Economic Area, 107
European Economic Community, 12
European Energy Community, 61
European Environmental Agency, 107
European integration, 3–4, 17, 21, 33, 50, 77, 104, 108, 114, 115, 117, 122; deepening, 4; widening, 4, 94
European security, 3, 12, 19, 51, 77, 95

European Security Treaty (proposed by Russia), 77
European Union (EU), accountability of the, 97, 110, 136; *acquis communautaire*, 17–18, 115; ambiguity of the, 6, 22, 23, 24, 64, 105; candidate for membership in the, 5, 11, 17, 18, 19, 24, 45, 57, 104 106; Common Agricultural Policy, 21, 46; conditionality and conditions of the, 17–18, 33, 36, 37, 40, 45, 47, 51, 54, 63, 72, 97, 98 104, 106, 112; Constitutional Treaty, 19–20; credibility of the, 38–40, 49, 65, 96, 100, 104; defense policy of the, 28, 32, 108; enlargement of the, 5–6, 17–19, 20, 22, 58, 92–94, 104; Erasmus program, 16; EU3 (on Iran), 108; Euro, 4; European Commission, 15, 41; European Neighborhood Policy, 23, 58, 87, 88, 129; European Parliament, 16; European Security Strategy, 6, 110; European Initiative for Democracy and Human Rights, 95; financial assistance, 5, 57, 84, 85, 87, foreign policy of, 5, 23, 61, 71, 77, 89, 105, 108; FRONTEX, 89; legitimacy, 8, 58, 110; membership in the, 5, 33, 36, 39, 48, 84, 87, 92, 97, 98, 99, 106, 107, 114, 134; public opinion about, 21
Europeanization, 7, 44, 71, 89, 94, 104
Euro-regions, 109
Eurovision Song Contest, 16
Ferdinand, Archduke Franz, 39
financial crisis, 7, 21, 70; in Ukraine, 64; in Russia, 75

Finland, 71, 83
Fischer, Joschka, 15
Florence, 112
France, 20, 56, 63, 71, 74, 80, 86, 100; and democracy assistance, 110–11; "empty chair" tactics, 12; French National Assembly, 48; *laïcité* in, 15, 44; response to EU Constitutional Treaty, 20

"freedom agenda," 110
Freedom House, 2

G 6, on immigration, 88
G 8, 74; Broader Middle East and
  North Africa Initiative, 96
gastarbeiter, 47
Gaza Strip, 86
Gazprom, 71, 76, 77, 114, 131
Gellner, Ernest, 30
geopolitics, 4, 19, 60
Georgia, 2, 54, 55, 61, 63; war with
  Russia, 56, 59, 74–75, 77
Georgia Tbilisi International Airport, 91
German Christian Democrats, 43
Germany, 20, 28, 30, 31, 32, 63, 70, 71,
  76, 82, 88, 107, 108, 109; nation-
  building in, 31; post-war economic
  growth in, 11; Turkish minority in,
  47
Gibraltar, Strait of, 79
Gulf of Finland, 83
globalization, 7, 22, 113
Gorbachev, Mikhail, 73, 96
Gorchakov, Aleksandr, 67, 68
Gotovina, General Ante, 36, 37
governance, 4, 14, 17–18, 19, 57, 58,
  60, 95, 96, 97, 103, 111, 115; good,
  55, 63, 97
Greece, 4, 31, 80, 126
Greenpeace, 113
Grotius, Hugo, 89
Gül, Abdullah, 42, 47
Gulf monarchies, 2

Habermas, Jürgen, 10, 14
headscarf, 81
Helsinki, 83
Holy Land, 86
human rights, 23, 84, 95, 106, 134;
  abuses/violations of 19, 24, 72
Hungary, 18, 53, 64, 99, 108

Iceland, 107
immigration, 1–2, 21, 24, 52, 82,
  88–89, 106, 107; Mediterranean,
  80–81; North African, 83; Slavic, 5;
  Turkish, 46–47

incentives (political and economic), 5,
  6, 12, 33, 36, 54, 58, 87, 98, 105, 106,
  112
India, 113
International Criminal Tribunal for
  the former Yugoslavia, 36–37, 39
International Monetary Fund, 45, 64
intifada, 85
Iran, 76, 87, 98, 108
Iraq, 15, 51, 74, 87, 91, 92, 93, 96, 97;
  nation-building in, 31; U.S.-led war
  in, 10, 19
Ireland, 11, 21, 107; Treaty of Nice,
  Ireland response to, 21
Islam, 3, 43, 82, 103; Islamism and
  political Islam, 43, 82–83, 97–98;
  Muslim world and societies, 3, 5,
  10, 38, 47, 50, 70, 80–84; Islamo-
  phobia, 82; radicalization, 82
Israel, 23, 85–86, 106, 108, 132
Istanbul, 50
Istiklal Avenue, 50
Italy, 3, 21, 31, 48, 50, 53, 71, 76, 80,
  88, 89, 107

Janus, 59
Japan, nation-building in, 31
Jordan, 23, 88, 98, 132, 133
Justice and Development Party
  (AKP), 42, 43–44, 45; of Morocco,
  82

Kaliningrad, 70
Kant, Immanuel, 15
Karadzic, Radovan, 28, 37
Kemal, Mustafa, 42–43
Kemalists, 43, 44
KGB (*Komitet Gosudarstvennoy
  Bezopasnosti*), 69
Kosovo, 28, 30, 32, 35, 37, 38, 91;
  supervised independence, 35
Kozyrev, Andrei, 72
Kurdistan Workers Party, 50

Lampedusa, 80
Latin America, 16, 94, 114, 115
Latvia, 18, 58, 64
Lebanon, 23, 82, 86, 88, 108, 132

Libya, 2, 23, 85, 89, 98, 111, 132, 133
Lithuania, 2, 18, 109, 111
Litvinenko, Aleksandr, 73
London, 69
Lukashenka, Aleksandr, 63

Macedonia (Former Yugoslav
  Republic of), 28, 29, 31, 32, 35, 125
Madrid, 83
Mahler, Gustav, 60, 63
Malta, 18
Mani and Manichaeism, 9
Mare Liberum, 89
Marshall Plan, 4, 11–12
Marshall Tito barracks, 27
Mediterranean region, 6, 7, 79–90;
  Arab-Israeli conflict and EU policy,
  85–86; devolution, awkward,
  87–89; European outlook in, 89–90;
  immigration, 80–81; Muslim
  population, 80–81; Muslim
  radicalization, 82
Medvedev, Dmitry, 70, 74
Mercado Común del Sur (Mercosur), 114
Merkel, Angela, 109, 123
Mesopotamia, 9
Mexico, 58
Middle Ages, 3, 16; neo-medieval
  metaphor, 16, 17, 18, 19, 22, 113
Middle East, 2, 7, 23, 51, 70, 81, 82,
  88, 90, 91, 94, 108, 111; "Quartet,"
  86 88; Partnership Initiative, 96, 100
Milakovic, Milorad, 31
Milosevic, Slobodan 28
minorities, in Europe 18, 44, 80, 84, 95;
  Russian-speaking, 73; in Turkey 45
Mladic, General Ratko, 37
Mohammed cartoons, 81
Moldova, 23, 54, 55, 59, 61, 105
Monnet, Jean, 12, 87
Montenegro, 28, 33, 37
Morocco, 1, 82, 84, 86, 88, 89, 105
movement of people, 88, 106
Mubarak, Hosni, 111
multipolar world order, 112

Nabucco pipeline, 76
Nagorno-Karabakh, 56

Naples, 31
National Endowment for Democracy,
  96
nationalism, 1, 11, 13, 25, 28, 29–30,
  32
nation-building, 31–32
NATO. *See* North Atlantic Treaty
  Organization
Netherlands, the, 80; response to EU
  Constitutional Treaty, 20
new democratic realism, 110, 112
nexus. *See* security and integration
Nicaragua, 74
Nigeria, 76
non-governmental organizations, 113
Nordic cooperation, 108
Nord Stream pipeline, 76
North Africa, 7, 23, 81, 91, 104, 111;
  immigration from or through, 1–2,
  80, 83, 89, political standards, 2,
  55, 79, 82, 90, 96; trade
  liberalization, 85
North Atlantic Treaty Organization
  (NATO), 11, 38, 51, 63, 68, 77, 93,
  94, 99; bombings over Serbia, 68;
  and energy security, 101;
  enlargement, 38, 55, 63–64, 98, 100;
  and the EU, 93, 94, 98–100;
  Mediterranean Dialogue, 100
Norway, 107
nuclear weapons, 14, 70

Obama, Barack, 12, 64, 92, 98, 101,
  123
oil shock, 11
Orange Revolution, 111
Organization for Security and
  Cooperation in Europe, 51
Orient Express, 41
Ottoman Empire, 42, 48

Palestinian Authority, 23, 86, 132
Patten, Chris, 69
Persian empire, 9
Peter the Great, Czar, 62
Platini, Michel, 53
Poland, 23, 29, 53, 73, 88, 96, 99, 108,
  109, 111

Polish plumber, 20, 22
Portugal, 4, 126
poverty, 1, 11, 24, 25, 30, 114
precautionary principle, 114
Pristina, 91
privatization, 55, 112
Prodi, Romano, 73, 129
protectorate, 2, 33, 35, 36
Putin, Vladimir, 68, 69, 70, 73, 74, 130, 131

Qaddafi, Muammar, 111
Qatar, 76
Quartet on the Middle East, 86, 88

Ratzinger, Joseph (Pope Benedict XVI), 103
realpolitik, 76, 94
Reform Treaty, 108; Ireland response to, 21
regional cooperation, 33, 61, 100, 109, 114–15
Rehn, Olli, 124, 127
relative powers, 113
relativism, 103
religion, 2, 9, 15, 47; and politics, 14, 43
Rio Grande, 80
Roman empire, 9
Romania, 18, 31, 39, 108
Rome, 50
Rousseau, Jean-Jacques, 70
Rumsfeld, Donald, 10
Russia, 2, 5, 38, 58, 67–78, 94, 100, 109, 113; Beslan school siege, 69; Common Spaces (EU-Russia document), 73; common values and, 72–73; and energy issues, 59, 76; European policy towards, 71, 76; European Security Treaty, 77; foreign policy views within, 71–72; neighborhood strategy of, 73; and "responsibility to protect," 74; revisionism, 73; "spinach treatment" of financial and economic reforms, 68; strategic partnership with the EU, 71; war with Georgia, 56, 59, 74–75, 77

Saakashvili, Mikhail, 56
Samos, 80
sanctions, 58, 59, 74, 98
Sarajevo, 27, 39
Sarkozy, Nicolas, 75, 87, 123, 131, 133, 136
Scarface, 31
Schröder, Gerhard, 76
Schuman, Robert, 12
secularism, 14, 25; in Turkey 42, 44
security and integration, 3–5, 6, 15, 17, 28, 33, 104, 110
Serbia, 28, 29, 30, 33, 35, 36, 37, 38, 68, 76; and Kosovo, 35; and the International Criminal Tribunal for the Former Yugoslavia, 36–37; and Russia, 38, 68, 76
Sharia law, 44
Siberian prisons, 69; tigers, 31
siloviki, 68
Slovakia, 11, 71, 108
Slovenia, 18
"Sniper Alley" (Sarajevo), 27
soccer, 11, 53
social contract, 38
Southern Europe, 4, 23, 80, 84, 88
South Ossetia, 56, 61, 75
South Stream project, 76
sovereignty, 35, 44, 94; sharing, 4, 12, 14, 29, 109, 113
Soviet Union, 29, 54, 55, 67, 71, 111; collapse of the, 4, 70, 73; former Soviet republics, *See* Eastern Europe
Spain, 3, 4, 21, 2, 72, 79, 80, 82, 88, 89, 107
Srpska Republic, 38
state-building, 32, 42
statelet, 2, 56, 74
Steinmeier, Frank Walter, 75
Stiftungen (German foundations), 96
students, 16, 39, 62
subsidiarity principle, 89
Sweden, 11, 23, and democracy assistance 110–11
Switzerland, 11, 107
Syria, 23, 98, 132
Taliban, 32

tax collection, 55–56, 70
terrorism, 3, 69, 82, 85, 107, 110;
    terrorist groups, 31, 69, 113
town twinning, 109
trade, 7, 39; barriers, 12, 105; "deep
    free", 60, 62, 105; free, 16, 60, 73,
    85, 86, 105; sanctions, 59
trafficking, 30, 31, 52, 55, 60; of
    human beings, 31, 106; of narcotics,
    30, 55, 125; of weapons, 31, 55
Train a Grande Vitesse (TGV), 41
transatlantic consensus, 91; on
    democracy, promotion, 95–97; on
    EU enlargement policy, 92–94; on
    conditionality, 97–99
transition, 5, 18, 33, 34, 39, 46, 54–57,
    58, 64, 68, 93, 95, 111
Transniestria, 56, 61
Transparency International
    Corruption Perception Index, 31
tribalism, 30
Tudjman, Franjo, 28
Tunisia, 23, 132, 133
Turkey, 1, 2, 3, 5, 22, 25, 41–52, 55, 81,
    87, 92, 94, 97, 99, 103, 106, 107;
    Armenian "genocide," 48; Article
    301, 44, 49; and Cyprus, 49, 99, 134;
    democracy, 47–48; *e*-coup, 42;
    "Euro-Turks," 47; and the
    International Monetary Fund, 45;
    Kurdish minority, 44;
    modernization, 42–45; negotiating
    framework with the EU, 46, 47;
    populism, 42; reform record, 45;
    safeguard clauses, 46, 106;
    secularism in, 42, 44;
    "Turkishness," 42, 44;
    westernization, 44
Turkish General Staff, 42

Ukraine, 2, 23, 53, 54, 58, 61, 62, 88,
    98, 99, 104, 105, 106, 108, 111, 129;
    and Colored Revolutions, 55; and
    energy issues, 59; and Euro-
    Atlantic integration, 63; prospective
    EU membership, 64
Union for the Mediterranean, 87–88

Union of European Football
    Associations (UEFA), 53
"United in Diversity," 15
United Kingdom, 11, 21, 23, 39, 50,
    73, 82, 88, 107, 108
United Nations, 31
United States of America, 28, 38, 90,
    91–101, 112, 113; democracy-
    promotion efforts, 95, 96; and
    Europe, 11–12; National Security
    Strategy of the, 95; relative decline,
    112; "war on terror," 10, 92, 110;
    USAID (US Agency for
    International Development), 112.
universities, 16, 20, 27, 39, 44

Vatican, 28
Vienna, siege of, 47; Congress of, 67
visa, 62, 73; regime revision, for
    Eastern European citizens, 62; visa-
    facilitation, 106; visa liberalization,
    106
Visegrad Group, 108
Volkswagens, 27
Walesa, Lech, 96

war, 1, 3, 9, 11, 12, 13, 14, 16, 17, 24,
    61; in the Balkans, 25, 31, 34, 36;
    civil, 97; crimes, 30; and democratic
    transition, 56; in Iraq, 10, 15, 51; on
    terror, 10, 92, 110
weapons of mass destruction, 98
Western Europe, 1, 12, 13, 14, 17, 82,
    124; anti-Americanism in, 10;
    economies of, 11, 13, 20; Russia
    policy of, 59.
White House, 115
"Window to Europe" (broadcast), 62
World Bank, 55, 85
world order, 112–15
World Trade Organization, 113
World War I, 42
World War II, 13, 32, 70, 114

Yeltsin, Boris, 68
Yugoslavia, 28, 29, 36
Yushchenko, Viktor, 111

About the Author

FABRIZIO TASSINARI is a Senior Fellow at the Danish Institute for International Studies. He is also an Associate Fellow at the Centre for European Policy Studies, Brussels, and non-resident Fellow at the Center for Transatlantic Relations at Johns Hopkins' School of Advanced International Studies, Washington, D.C. Dr. Tassinari has published extensively on issues pertaining to European integration and security. Previously, he worked as a researcher in a European Union–financed research network coordinated by Humboldt University, Berlin, and was Assistant Professor of Political Science at the University of Copenhagen.